Are you right with God?

"Wisdom That Transforms. Action That Lasts."

The Get Wisdom Commitment

At Get Wisdom Publishing we believe that true wisdom has the power to transform lives. Our mission is to equip readers with timeless insights and practical tools that inspire growth, guide decisions, and empower purposeful living. We don't just inform—we empower.

Our books combine profound understanding with real-life application, enabling readers to unlock their potential and navigate life's challenges with clarity and confidence. With each step guided by wisdom, we help you create lasting change and live the life you deserve.

When wisdom meets purpose, transformation follows.

Copyright

The RELATIONSHIP CHARACTERISTICS of a Jesus Follower: Are You Right With God? by Stephen H Berkey, published by Get Wisdom Publishing, Box 465, Thompsons Station, TN 37179, copyright © 2024, Stephen H Berkey

All rights reserved. No portion of this book may be reproduced in any form without written permission from the publisher, except as permitted by U.S. copyright law. For permission contact: info@getwisdompublishing.com

Scriptures marked ESV are taken from THE HOLY BIBLE, ENGLISH STANDARD VERSION® Copyright© 2001 by Crossway, a publishing ministry of Good News Publishers. Used by permission.

Scriptures marked NLT are taken from the HOLY BIBLE, NEW LIVING TRANSLATION, copyright© 1996, 2004, 2007 by Tyndale House Foundation. Used by permission of Tyndale House Publishers, Inc., Carol Stream, Illinois 60188. All rights reserved. Used by permission.

Scriptures marked HCSB or HOLMAN are taken from the HOLMAN CHRISTIAN STANDARD BIBLE (HCSB): Scripture taken from the HOLMAN CHRISTIAN STANDARD BIBLE, copyright© 1999, 2000, 2002, 2003 by Holman Bible Publishers, Nashville Tennessee. All rights reserved.

Scriptures marked NIV are taken from the NEW INTERNATIONAL VERSION (NIV): Scripture taken from THE HOLY BIBLE, NEW INTERNATIONAL VERSION ®. Copyright© 1973, 1978, 1984, 2011 by Biblica, Inc.™. Used by permission of Zondervan

ISBN 978-1-952359-58-3   (paperback)
ISBN 978-1-952359-59-0   (ebook)

This book is available as an audiobook on our Amazon Jesus Follower Series page:

Unlock Biblical Wisdom and Transform Your Faith

**For more information
about the Jesus Follower Bible Study Series:**
https://getwisdompublishing.com/jesus-follower-series/

Jesus Follower Bible Study Series

The RELATIONSHIP CHARACTERISTICS of a Jesus Follower

Are You Right With God?

Stephen H Berkey

GETWISDOM PUBLISHING

This book is available as an audiobook on our Amazon Jesus Follower Series page:

Are you right with God?

Free PDF
Living Wisely

The Life Planning Guide

> *A Quick-Start Guide to Purposeful Living and Wise Decisions!*
>
> Discover the five life domains: purpose, people, principles, productivity, and perspective. Wisdom is the ability to apply truth and logic to real-life decisions and produce good outcomes. It influences your choices and will produce action that lasts. Consider and apply the five practical wisdom principles for daily living. (6 pages)
>
> **Free PDF:** https://getwisdompublishing.com/resource-registration/

Free PDF

Five Practical Principles For Life

When wisdom meets purpose, transformation follows.

Are you right with God?

Free PDF
Wise Decision-Making

[Get the ebook version for 99 cents]

> ***You can make good choices.***
>
> **This free resource provides a project-oriented perspective and gives ten detailed steps to analyze issues/problems to determine a solution. (26 pages)**
>
> Good decisions expand your horizons. Don't allow the fear of decision-making paralyze your ability to make good choices. Think through the reasonable alternatives and move forward. When your eyes are on the goal, making good decisions is easier.
>
> **Free PDF:** https://getwisdompublishing.com/resource-registration/
>
> **Kindle ebook for 99 cents:** https://www.amazon.com/dp/B09SYGWRVL/

Ebook

Free PDF

Make Thoughtful Decisions!

Good decisions expand your horizons

Effective Life Change
Applying Biblical Wisdom to Live Your Best Life!

Why Read This Book?

- Transform Your life with Biblical Wisdom.
- Cultivate Practical Wisdom in Your life.
- Navigate Life with a Perspective on Biblical Truth.
- Unlock the Proverbs of the Bible to Live Your Best Life.
- Change and Transform Your life.

   Practical Application: These aren't theology or religious discussions, they're practical tools for everyday living.

Get Your Copy Today!

https://www.amazon.com/dp/1952359732
Available in Hardcover, Paperback, Kindle, and Audiobook.

The Jesus Follower Journey
Jesus Follower Bible Study Series

The Jesus Follower Bible Study Series will provide you with a complete description of the nature, characteristics, obligations, commitments, and responsibilities of a true Jesus follower.

Go to our Amazon Book Series page for your copy:
https://www.amazon.com/dp/B0DHP39P5J

The RELATIONSHIP CHARACTERISTICS of a Jesus Follower:
    Are you right with God?
The ONE ANOTHER INSTRUCTIONS to a Jesus Follower:
    Are you right with one another?
The WORSHIP of a Jesus Follower:
    Is your worship acceptable or in vain?
The PRAYER of a Jesus Follower:
    What Scripture says about unleashing the power of God.
The DANGERS of SIN for a Jesus Follower:
    God HATES sin! He abhors sin!
The FOCUS for a Jesus Follower:
    Keep your eyes fixed on Jesus!
The HEART Requirements of a Jesus Follower:
    Follow with all your heart, mind, body, and soul!
The COMMITMENTS of a Jesus Follower:
    Practical Christian living and discipleship.
The OBEDIENCE Requirements for a Jesus Follower:
    Ignore at your own risk!

A related book to this series is, *Effective Life Change: Applying Biblical Wisdom to Live Your Best Life!* This book offers a practical and powerful guide to help navigate life's challenges based on the proverbial wisdom of the Bible. It offers ten commitments hat will profoundly change your life.

Are you right with God?

Table of Contents

Copyright 2

Free PDF Living Wisely 4

Free PDF Wise Decision-Making 5

Effective Life Change 6

Jesus Follower Bible Study Series 7

Table of Contents 8

Message From the Author 10

Introduction 13

Lesson 1 Being Loved by God 15

Lesson 2 A Relationship with God 23

Lesson 3 Being Available to God 38

Lesson 4 Pursuing and Seeking God 49

Lesson 5 Abiding in God 59

Lesson 6 Knowing God 71

Lesson 7 Loving God 81

Lesson 8 Obeying God 94

Lesson 9 Depend on and Trust God 106

Lesson 10   Walk Humbly With Your God 117

Lesson 11 Enjoy God 130

Lesson 12 Worship God 142

Appendix A   Quiet Time 155
Appendix B How To Study The Bible................................... 156
Appendix C What I Want To Remember............................. 157
Appendix D Relationship Life Plan 159

Transformation Road Map.. 161
Leader Guide... 163
Free PDF MAKE WISE DECISIONS... 180
Free PDF Life Improvement Principles................................. 181
What Next? 182
The OBSCURE Bible Study Series 183
Life Planning Series 184
Personal Daily Prayer Guide 185
Acknowledgments 186
Notes... 186
About the Author... 187
Contact Us... 188

Message From the Author

Dear Fellow Christ follower,

Welcome to a journey of faith and discovery.

As the author of this Bible study series, I am excited about the future because I believe this book provides the potential to transform lives, deepen our understanding of God's Word, and ignite a desire within us—a fire that draws us into the presence of our God.

Why read the Jesus Follower Series?

Deeper Roots: We all long for roots that run deep—roots anchored in truth, love, and purpose. In this series, we'll dig into the bedrock of Scripture, unearthing spiritual principles that will guide us in our faith journey.

Authentic Discipleship: Being a Jesus follower isn't about rituals or a superficial commitment. It's about walking the narrow path, picking up your cross, and living a life that loves God, follows Jesus, and loves one another. We will explore what it means to be authentic disciples.

Unveiling Mysteries: God is a source of mysteries and His Word is waiting to be discovered. Together we will examine and encounter the living Word—the One who breathes life into every syllable.

Community and Connection: We are not meant to walk this path alone. As you read, imagine joining a global community of fellow seekers. We will discuss, question, and grow together. Our shared journey will enrich us all. I encourage you to gather friends to join you in this journey.

Expected Benefits:

Renewed Passion: Prepare yourself to wake up each morning with a renewed passion for God's Word. These studies will ignite your hunger for truth and draw you into deeper relationship with the Author of Life.

Practical Application: These aren't theoretical discussions; they're practical tools for everyday living. Expect to see real-life changes—whether it's in your relationships, commitment, or prayer life.

Spiritual Resilience: Life's storms will come, but armed with the insights from God's Word, you can stand firm. Your faith will weather trials, doubts, and uncertainties. You will emerge stronger and more resilient.

Joyful Obedience: As we explore the nature of discipleship, you'll discover that obedience isn't a burden—it's a joy. The path of obedience leads to peace, and you'll find yourself saying, "Yes, Lord!" with newfound delight.

Let's Begin!

So, turn the page. Dive into the first chapter. Let the words seep into your soul. And remember, you're not alone—we're on this pilgrimage together. May these books be more than ink on paper; may they be stepping stones toward a life that leads to eternity. Amen!

> *"We believe applied wisdom empowers life change. Our books provide clarity, inspiration, and tools to equip readers to live their best life."*

Are you right with God?

My prayer is that you will

Be tenacious like Job
Walk like Enoch
Believe like Abraham
Wrestle like Jacob
Dress like Joseph
Lead like Moses
Conquer like Deborah
Be fearless like Shamgar
Inspire like Josuha
Influence like Esther
Dance like David
Ask like Jabez
Have the faith of Daniel
Pray like Elijah
Trust like Elisha
Commit like Isaiah
Be courageous like Benaiah
Rebuild like Nehemiah
Be obedient like Hosea
Be zealous like Zacchaeus
Surrender like Mary
Stand firm like Stephen
Speak like Peter
Seize opportunities like Philip
Submit like Paul
Overcome like the Elect (Saints)
Worship like the 24 Elders
and
Love like Jesus

Steve

Introduction

The life of a Jesus follower is first and foremost characterized by an intimate, growing, love relationship with God.

Book Description

Are you ready to deepen your relationship with Christ? "The Jesus Follower Bible Study" invites you on a transformative journey to discover what it truly means to be a follower of Jesus. This isn't just another study; it's a heartfelt exploration into the very essence of discipleship and the life-changing power of faith. This book addresses the fundamental question, "What does it mean to be a true Jesus follower?" If I claim to follow Jesus, then what should my life look like? How should I act? What should I do?

In today's world, it's easy to claim to follow Jesus, but what does that really look like in our daily lives? Through twelve compelling lessons, you will uncover the essential characteristics that define a vibrant relationship with God:

- **Being Loved by God**: Embrace the profound truth that you are loved by your Creator.
- **A Relationship with God**: Cultivate a deep, personal connection with your Savior.
- **Being Available to God**: Learn to prioritize God's will in your daily life.
- **Pursuing and Seeking God**: Ignite your passion for a deeper walk with the Lord.
- **Abiding in God**: Learn the importance of staying connected to the source of your strength.
- **Knowing God**: Gain a deeper understanding of God's character and nature.
- **Loving God**: Experience the joy of loving God with all your heart.

- **Obeying God**: Understand the importance of obedience in your walk with Christ.
- **Depend on and Trust God**: Build unwavering trust in God's plan for your life.
- **Walk Humbly With Your God**: Embrace humility as a cornerstone of your faith.
- **Enjoy God**: Discover the joy and delight that come from a relationship with God.
- **Worship God**: Elevate your worship to new heights of intimacy and reverence.

Grounded firmly in Scripture, this study prioritizes the wisdom of the Bible over personal opinions or theories. It's an invitation to not only learn but to experience God in a profound way, but it will transform your understanding of what it means to follow Jesus.

Whether you are a new believer seeking guidance or a seasoned follower looking to rekindle your faith, "The Jesus Follower Bible Study" offers tools, insights, and encouragement to help you flourish in your spiritual journey. Dig into this study, and let the transformative power of God's Word illuminate your path as you grow in your relationship with Him.

Your journey begins here. Take the first step toward a life filled with purpose, love, and divine connection.

Group Discussion or Individual Study

These studies can be done individually or in a small discussion group. An important value of the study is in the discussion questions. We all see life differently and the thoughts and ideas shared in a group will often lead to a richer understanding of the Scripture. We recommend doing these studies in a group, if possible.

The format of the lessons is not the same in each book. We chose a format that best fit the material.

Lesson 1
Being Loved by God

The life of a Jesus follower can be identified by a number of characteristics describing the nature of his relationship with God. These are not performance activities, but relationship characteristics. They are the stepping stones to establishing, building, and cementing an intimate love relationship with Jesus.

LESSON MEDITATION

Meditate on Psalm 103 during your Quiet Time this week. Consider making a list of what God has done for you.

DEFINITIONS - LOVE

In the non-biblical world "love" is generally thought to be strong feelings of affection. Such love is the result of admiration, romantic feelings, benevolence, or common personal interests. It can be described as devotion or thought of as simple unconditional concern for the well-being of another.

Biblically, love is often associated with God's concern for His creation, particularly man. It can also be described as high esteem or high regard. Love is often considered the most important attribute of God.

Love is not only one of God's attributes it is an essential part of His nature. The Bible declares that "God is love" (1 John 4:8, 16). He is the personification of perfect love. Such love surpasses our powers of understanding (Eph 3:19). Love like this is everlasting (Jer 31:3), free (Hos 14:4), sacrificial (John 3:16), and enduring to the end (John 13:1).

Two distinct Greek words for love appear in the Bible. The word *phileo* means "to have ardent affection and feeling." It is a type of impulsive love. The other word, *agapao,* means "to have esteem" or "high regard." In the memorable conversation between Jesus and Peter, there is a play upon these two words (John 21:15-17). Jesus asked, "Simon, do you love [esteem] me?" But Peter replied, "You know that I love [have ardent affection for] You." Then Jesus asked, "Simon, do you love [have ardent affection for] Me?" And Peter responded that his love was agape love – a love that held Jesus in high esteem and that was more than a fleeting feeling.[1]

Some interpretations suggest that Jesus was challenging Peter to a deeper commitment and sacrificial love, urging him to move beyond mere affection to a selfless devotion. Others see it as a compassionate acknowledgment of Peter's current state, understanding that Peter's love was genuine but perhaps not yet fully matured into the selfless love Jesus wanted from him.

Overall, this exchange highlights themes of love, commitment, and discipleship, inviting believers to examine the nature of their own love for God and one another and to aspire to embody the sacrificial love exemplified by Jesus.

Q1. What evidence can you suggest to demonstrate or prove that God loves you?

OBSERVATIONS

Q2. What do you learn or observe in the following verses?

John 15:9 *As the Father has loved me, so have I loved you. Abide in my love.* ESV

Deuteronomy 7:6-8 *For you are a people holy to the Lord your God. The Lord your God has chosen you to be a people for his treasured possession, out of all the peoples who are on the face of the earth. 7 It was not because you were more in number than any other people that the Lord set his love on you and chose you, for you were the fewest of all peoples, 8 but it is because the Lord loves you...* ESV

Q3. What does it mean to be a "treasured possession"?

John 15:16 *You did not choose me, but I chose you and appointed you that you should go and bear fruit and that your fruit should abide, so that whatever you ask the Father in my name, he may give it to you.* ESV

John 15:13 *Greater love has no one than this, that someone lays down his life for his friends.* ESV

Q4. Are any of the verses above troubling for you or hard to believe?

Q5. How might you summarize the above relative to God's love?

Q6. What do you learn from the following passage about God's love?

Romans 8:35-39 *Who shall separate us from the love of Christ? Shall tribulation, or distress, or persecution, or famine, or nakedness, or danger, or sword? . . . nor anything else in all creation, will be able to separate us from the love of God in Christ Jesus our Lord.* ESV

BENEFITS OF GOD'S LOVE

Q7. What benefits can you identify in the following verses?

Zephaniah 3:17 *The Lord your God is in your midst, a mighty one who will save; he will rejoice over you with gladness; he will quiet you by his love; he will exult over you with loud singing.* ESV

Romans 5:8 *. . . but God shows his love for us in that while we were still sinners, Christ died for us.* ESV

Q8. Does Ro 5:8 above seem plausible? Does it defy logic? What organizations accept you without some qualification?

Ephesians 2:4-5 *But God, being rich in mercy, because of the great love with which he loved us, 5 even when we were dead in our trespasses, made us alive together with Christ— by grace you have been saved.* ESV

Ephesians 3:19 *. . . and to know the love of Christ that surpasses knowledge, that you may be filled with all the fullness of God.* ESV

1 John 3:1 *See what kind of love the Father has given to us, that we should be called children of God . . .* ESV

1 John 4:12 *No one has ever seen God; if we love one another, God abides in us and his love is perfected in us.* ESV

1 John 4:8-10 *Anyone who does not love does not know God, because God is love. 9 In this the love of God was made manifest among us, that God sent his only Son into the world, so that we might live through him. 10 In this is love, not that we have loved God but that he loved us and sent his Son to be the propitiation for our sins.* ESV

Q9. Have you ever experienced any of the benefits described above?

If so, would you share your testimony with your group?

REFLECTION/OBSERVATION

Q10. In the space provided list at least three things God has done or is doing for us as recorded in Ro 8:31-34:

Romans 8:31-34 God's Everlasting Love
What then shall we say to these things? If God is for us, who can be against us? 32 He who did not spare his own Son but gave him up for us all, how will he not also with him graciously give us all things? 33 Who shall bring any charge against God's elect? It is God who justifies. 34 Who is to condemn? Christ Jesus is the one who died – more than that, who was raised – who is at the right hand of God, who indeed is interceding for us. ESV

1.

2.

3.

4.

5.

Q11. How do you react to the above? You must be somebody special! Do you feel special? What are your thoughts when you consider what God has done and Jesus is still doing?

Note: God's love is not a one way street – we must receive or accept it. We must know that His love exists and that it is available. God's love must be accepted (just like salvation) for it to be effective in our lives. We can talk about it, maybe even acknowledge it, but if it is not received, the knowledge of it is of little use to a Christ follower.

Q12. In *your life* what are some of the things you do that stifles or hinders God's love being poured out into your life?

Q13. To what degree have you or are you currently acknowledging and accepting God's love in your life?

Q14. In <u>your</u> opinion what are the three most important characteristics of a person who successfully acknowledges and receives God's love?

1.

2.

3.

Q15. What is the <u>key</u> ingredient for <u>you</u> in making God's love real in <u>your</u> life?

CONCLUSION

The concept that "God is love" boggles my mind! I have enough trouble with just the fact that God would love me at all. The best I can do is to suggest that God's love permeates all of His other attributes. He is faithful in love, He provides mercy in love, He disciplines in love, He administers justice with love, He exacts His wrath with love, etc.

If God loves me in my sinful condition, then I am compelled to love Him back and to love others, but I can do that only if I stay connected to Him in *relationship*. I must abide in Him because I'm not very good at doing it on my own. We will cover "abiding" in depth in a later lesson.

Prayer: Lord, give me the ability and courage to love You and others as you love me.

My Personal Prayer

What I Want to Remember

Enter some notes and information that you want to remember about this lesson. It might be a Scripture verse or two, something new you learned, something you want to do, something you want to change, or just something you want to be sure to remember.

Wisdom to Action
Challenge

Reflect on your interactions this week. How can you demonstrate God's unconditional love in a specific situation or relationship where it's challenging to do so?

Lesson 2
A Relationship with God

The life of a Jesus follower can be identified by a number of characteristics describing the nature of his relationship with God. These are not performance activities, but relationship characteristics. They are the stepping stones to establishing, building, and cementing an intimate love relationship with Jesus.

LESSON MEDITATION:

Meditate on Job's relationship with God during your Quiet Time this week:

> **Job 1:8** *And the Lord said to Satan, "Have you considered my servant Job, that there is none like him on the earth, a blameless and upright man, who fears God and turns away from evil?"* ESV

Think about the words of Jesus in the following: *So Jesus said to the Jews who had believed in him, "If you abide in my word, you are truly my disciples . . ."* (John 8:31 ESV)

INTRODUCTION

A member of a certain church, who previously had been attending services regularly, stopped going. After a few weeks, the preacher decided to visit him. It was a chilly evening. The preacher found the man at home alone, sitting before a blazing fire. Guessing the reason for his preacher's visit, the man welcomed him, led him to a comfortable chair near the fireplace and waited.

The preacher made himself at home but said nothing. In the grave silence, he contemplated the dance of the flames around the burning logs. After some minutes, the preacher took the fire tongs, carefully picked up a brightly burning ember and placed it to one side of the hearth all alone then he sat back in his chair, still silent. The host watched all this in quiet contemplation. As the one lone ember's flame flickered and diminished, there was a momentary glow and then its fire was no more. Soon it was cold and dead.

Not a word had been spoken since the initial greeting. The preacher glanced at his watch and realized it was time to leave. He slowly stood up, picked up the cold, dead ember and placed it back in the middle of the fire. Immediately it began to glow, once more with the light and warmth of the burning coals around it.

As the preacher reached the door to leave and with a tear running down his cheek, his host said, "Thank you so much for your visit and especially for the fiery sermon. I shall be back in church next Sunday."[2]

This story describes the meaning and nature of relationship. That is the focus in this week's lesson. In order to have a complete relationship with God through Christ, we need to be right with God, one another, and the world. This book focuses on the first of those relationships: being right with God.

RELATIONSHIP

The secular definition of relationship describes the way we talk and act with each other – how we interact. It's the way we are connected. It might be described as the nature of our kinship or association with each other.

The Biblical definition is a bit more complicated and is our focus for the rest of this lesson.

We have said that the life of a Jesus follower is first and foremost characterized by an intimate, growing, love relationship with God. The entire basis for this book rests on the truth of that premise. Thus, before we examine relationship characteristics we should understand that we are in fact called into a relationship and understand the nature of that relationship.

The word "relationship" appears only once in the NIV in Ro 2:17 (The NASB translates the text "relation"). The NLT translates the text as:

> *You who call yourselves Jews are relying on God's law, and you boast about your <u>special relationship</u> with him.*
> Romans 2:17 NLT

The word relationship does not appear in the ESV and in the verse above it says: "boast in God and know His will and approve what is excellent."

Thus, if we are really called into a relationship with Christ, we must see what other words the Bible uses to describe the result of this calling because this one use would not warrant concluding that a relationship was a critical ingredient in our faith. Further study confirms that the Bible does, in fact, use other terms to describe relationship. For example:

- **Fellowship** (fellowship is an almost identical word for relationship)
- **Disciple** (by definition it includes being in a relationship; this term is the one most often used to describe a follower)
- **Follow** (Jesus asked people to "follow" Him)
- **With Him** (Jesus wanted followers to be "with Him")
- **Family** (being a follower is to be in the family of God)
- **Slave** (God referred to Job as His servant and Paul described himself as a slave or servant of Christ)

All of these words indicate the desire of God for relationship with His people. How often are these words used? What is said about the importance and nature of all these terms that would be helpful to us before we examine the characteristics that define that relationship?

KNOWING CHRIST

When one compares Christianity to other expressions of faith, it is currently fashionable to say that Christianity is not a *religion* but a *relationship* with God or Jesus. Usually what is meant is that Christianity is not based on a set of qualifying rules but on the acceptance of Christ by faith and receipt of His grace. All other religions require that participants *earn* their way into heaven, but Jesus followers enter through faith in Christ who paid our sin debt with His shed blood, not by performing works.

From a Christ follower's perspective then, I can't earn my way into heaven or into God's favor because that's not the requirement. The requirement is a *relationship*, not a list of accomplishments or a standard of behavior that must be achieved to be considered "saved." This is dramatically illustrated by a passage in Scripture that can be very frightening if not understood correctly:

Matthew 7:21-23 I Never Knew You
"Not everyone who says to me, 'Lord, Lord,' will enter the kingdom of heaven, but the one who does the will of my Father who is in heaven. 22 On that day many will say to me, 'Lord, Lord, did we not prophesy in your name, and cast out demons in your name, and do many mighty works in your name?' 23 And then will I declare to them, 'I never knew you; depart from me, you workers of lawlessness.' ESV

Here we have someone who prophesied in Jesus' name, drove out demons, and performed many miracles, but did not have a personal relationship with the Lord. Jesus says, "I never knew you." At first glance one might conclude that if a person who does all this (in Jesus' name) still cannot get into heaven, what chance do I have? But the issue is not this man's performance activity. The problem is that he did <u>not</u> have a relationship with Christ, because Christ did not know him.

In many ways this understanding (interpretation, if you will) is a great relief to me, because my own performance activity leaves a lot to be desired. This passage confirms the foundational calling on all Jesus followers: I am a Christian because I have a personal relationship with God through Christ. Now, I do not mean to imply that Jesus followers do not do good works. We do them out of the overflow or excess of the love relationship that develops with Christ. Such works are not a requirement in order that Jesus "knows" me; rather, they are acts of gratitude performed because I am grateful and thankful that God's justice has been replaced with His grace.

The bottom line is that it does not matter how many good deeds you do or how spectacular they might be (e.g. casting our demons), if you have no personal relationship with Christ the doors to the Kingdom are not open to you. Therefore, first and foremost, we must be concerned that Jesus knows us – that we have a _relationship_ with Him.

The story of the Ten Virgins (Mt 25:1-13) uses similar language. When the virgins returned from getting more oil the door was closed. The bridegroom [Jesus] said he did not _know_ them. Therefore, _knowing Christ_ is an absolutely essential factor in our Christian walk. Otherwise we are in danger of being turned away because there is no relationship – He doesn't know us. The "knowing" that is described here is heart knowledge, not head knowledge. It implies relationship and experiencing God. God knows me because I am up every morning talking to Him in prayer and He in turn is talking to me through His Word.

The importance of knowing God did not start in the New Testament. In the book of Jeremiah we find this passage about boasting:

> **Jeremiah 9:23-24** _Thus says the Lord: "Let not the wise man boast in his wisdom, let not the mighty man boast in his might, let not the rich man boast in his riches, 24 but let him who boasts boast in this, that he understands and knows me, that I am the Lord who practices steadfast love, justice, and righteousness in the earth. For in these things I delight, declares the Lord." ESV_

This is pretty definitive. God says that if you are going to boast about anything, boast about knowing Me. My life is what it is because Christ is in my life. Nothing else really matters because my home is not on this earth. I am just traveling through this life for a short time and the only thing of value I possess is my relationship with Christ, and that He knows me.

> _And this is eternal life, that they know you the only true God, and Jesus Christ whom you have sent._
> John 17:3 ESV

Jesus makes the benefit of knowing God (Christ) very important when He ties *knowing Him* to eternal life. My ultimate hope is that eternal relationship!

FOLLOW ME

Jesus did not call the people directly to faith by grace but to follow Him and repent. His invitation to be a disciple was not about serving, working, or preaching. It was to repent and *follow* Him. Other than the obvious meaning to walk with or trail after, the Greek word means "to be in the same way with" [e.g. a disciple]. Jesus was inviting them to come along with Him and "buy into His program." He wanted people He could mold into disciples – people growing in knowledge and relationship with Him.

We find throughout the four gospels that Jesus called disciples to *follow* Him:

> **Matthew 4:19** *And he said to them, "Follow me, and I will make you fishers of men."* ESV
>
> **Matthew 16:24** *Then Jesus told his disciples, "If anyone would come after me, let him deny himself and take up his cross and follow me."* ESV
>
> **John 10:27-28** *My sheep hear my voice, and I know them, and they follow me. 28 I give them eternal life, and they will never perish, and no one will snatch them out of my hand.* ESV

Q1. What do we learn from the three verses above about the people who follow Jesus?

Mt 4:19

Mt 16:24

Jn 10:27-28

Jesus is obviously not talking about physically following Him around. The Matthew passages indicate there will be both work and a serious commitment required. John talks more about the relationship aspects using the metaphor of sheep describing the followers and the nature of the relationship: they are known by Him; they are safe and secure.

FELLOWSHIP

The second example of His calling us to relationship is the word "fellowship." Paul states it very plainly in 1 Cor 1:9 where he says, "God, who has called you into fellowship with his Son Jesus Christ our Lord, is faithful." And in 1 John 1:3 it says that, "our fellowship is with the Father and with his Son, Jesus Christ." The Greek word used here is "*koinonia*" which means "joint participation; partnership; or having things in common." The usage of the word approaches the common usage of today, that of fellowship and companionship. In Philippians 2:1 and 2 Corinthians 13:14 the word refers to the joint participation of the believer and the Holy Spirit in a common interest and activity in the things of God. Paul describes the depth of the fellowship or relationship with God as follows:

> **Romans 8:38-39** *For I am sure that neither death nor life, nor angels nor rulers, nor things present nor things to come, nor powers, 39 nor height nor depth, nor anything else in all creation, will be able to <u>separate us from the love of God</u> in Christ Jesus our Lord.* ESV

John speaks further about the fundamental nature of fellowship (or relationship):

> **1 John 1:4-6** *And we are writing these things so that our joy may be complete. 5 This is the message we have heard from him and proclaim to you, that God is light, and in him is no darkness at all. 6 If we say we have <u>fellowship</u> with him while we walk in darkness, we lie and do not practice the truth.* ESV

Life in Christ is such that if we are living in sin (walking in darkness) we cannot claim to truly know Him. This verse describes the connection as fellowship – we don't really have the fundamental requirement of being a Christ follower if we do not have fellowship, or a relationship, with Him. John's relationship with Jesus was personal and first-hand. He experienced Jesus and His teaching. John said that he had seen, heard, and touched Jesus and because of that John wrote his letter so others who wanted to be followers could have the same kind of fellowship with John and the other disciples.

Koinonia can be experienced with God only if one has a real relationship with God through Christ.

Q2. How would you describe the nature of your current relationship with Christ or God?

Spend time on this question because it will provide an excellent marker against which to compare at the end of this study.

Interestingly enough, once we have fellowship with Jesus we also have fellowship with one another, and that is another characteristic of our relationship with Him – it extends and broadens to include the entire family of God.

WITH HIM

John reports in his gospel that Jesus wants followers to be <u>with</u> Him. This language certainly adds to our understanding that Jesus is calling us into a relationship because He wants us to be with Him. Mark also uses this description in Mk 3:14 when he describes Jesus calling the twelve apostles saying, "that they might be with him." John emphasizes this concept by stating it three times:

> **John 14:3** *And if I go and prepare a place for you, I will come again and will take you to myself, that <u>where I am you may be also</u>.* ESV
>
> **John 14:16** *And I will ask the Father, and he will give you another Helper, to be <u>with you</u> forever . . .* ESV
>
> **John 17:24** *Father, I desire that they also, whom you have given me, may be <u>with me</u> where I am, to see my glory that you have given me because you loved me before the foundation of the world.* ESV

Being with Jesus in these verses means physical presence. He is not talking about some weird spiritual connection but an environment where real relationship and fellowship will occur. In John 14:3 Jesus says that He wants a physical relationship to the point that He will come back and take us to be with Him. And He confirms that desire for physical presence as part of His prayer in John 17:24. Relationship is very important to Jesus, and in this context it is being described as physical presence.

For three years Jesus spent time with His disciples. They were together constantly. Jesus wanted it that way so they could observe Him and He could interact with them and teach them. The disciples could observe Jesus first-hand and get to know Him personally – because they were <u>with Him</u>. He calls us to discipleship so that we can also be with Him and know Him.

If we are good enough at something to warrant boasting (Jeremiah 9:23-24 referenced earlier), it means that we have become very good at what we are boasting about. God tells us through Jeremiah that we should be very good at knowing and understanding God – because if we are going to boast, it ought to be about Him – not about our golf game, our jobs, our family, but about the most important person in our lives . . . God!

And Jesus says He wants that to happen by being with us.

BEING A DISCIPLE

Rather than to call people to follow Him, Jesus could have invited them to be disciples. I am sure there is probably some technical difference between a follower and a disciple, but for our purposes that difference is probably not significant. The Bible says little about the nature of followers except in relation to Jesus' calling the Twelve to follow Him. The Bible does have much to say about disciples. In fact, this is the term most often used in the New Testament to describe a follower. It occurs more than 250 times. Therefore it is important to understand the nature, character, and calling of a disciple.

We define a disciple as a person growing in his or her relationship with Christ Jesus, who is eager to learn and apply the truth of the Word of God in his or her life, resulting in a deeper commitment to a Christ-like lifestyle and service.

In the Book of John, Jesus pointed out three characteristics of a real believer or a real disciple:

> **John 8:31** . . . *If you abide in my word, you are truly my disciples* . . . ESV
>
> **John 13:35** *By this all people will know that you are my disciples, if you have love for one another.* ESV
>
> **John 15:8** *By this my Father is glorified, that you bear much fruit and so prove to be my disciples.* ESV

One might describe these three characteristics as, *obey, connect, and share*. The Biblical teaching about disciples makes it clear that being a disciple involves action. We can't consider ourselves a disciple if we are not actively growing in Christ and participating in church. We must be developing and growing in our relationship with Jesus in order to do that.

In the Great Commission we could easily replace the words, "make disciples" with "call followers." We are actually asking seekers to do the same thing Jesus asked when He called His disciples to follow Him. We ask them to accept and follow the Lord, and then we teach them about faith.

Our definition of a disciple says that we have a *growing relationship* with Christ. In other words, we have come to understand that it is not about "religion," it's about a personal evolving relationship with Jesus. Thus, we seek to learn all we can about Him, spending time with Him, and then take that knowledge to the next level by applying it to our lives.

SLAVE

The Bible uses the words "slave" and "servant" in two very different ways throughout Scripture. The Bible clearly teaches in John 8:34 that we are slaves to sin: "I say to you, everyone who commits sin is a slave to sin." (also see Ro 7:14, 25) Sin can hold us in bondage and life can be very difficult when we are struggling with a sin we cannot shake.

Let's first examine the word "slave" as it is used to describe the nature of our relationship with Christ. Paul labeled the nature of his apostolic relationship as being that of a *slave or servant* to Christ:

> Ro 1:1   Paul, a <u>servant</u> of Christ Jesus . . .
> Phil 1:1   Paul and Timothy, <u>servants</u> of Christ Jesus . . .
> Gal 1:10   . . . I would not be a <u>servant</u> of Christ.

Those who call themselves a slave to Christ acknowledge that Jesus (the Godhead) should and will control their life, set their direction, and determine their future. I might say simply that Jesus has power over me. A more accurate way to think about it, however, is that I have submitted or surrendered my life to Jesus. He sits on the throne of my life and I follow His direction without question because I totally trust Him. I live in obedience because I choose to. That's more easily said than done – unless the relationship is personal, intimate, and tested.

Several scriptures indicate that our "slave relationship" is in the nature of a son and not one of bondage:

> **John 8:35-36** *The <u>slave</u> does not remain in the house forever; the son remains forever. 36 So if the Son sets you free, you will be free indeed.* ESV

> **Galatians 4:7** *So you are no longer a <u>slave</u>, but a son, and if a son, then an heir through God.* ESV

> **Romans 8:15** *For you did not receive the spirit of <u>slavery</u> to fall back into fear, but you have received the Spirit of adoption as sons, by whom we cry, "Abba! Father!"* ESV

Jesus confirms the existence of this servant or slave relationship in the following:

> **John 12:26** *If anyone serves me, he must follow me; and where I am, there will my <u>servant</u> be also. If anyone serves me, the Father will honor him.* ESV

> **Matthew 8:9** *For I too am a man under authority, with soldiers under me. And I say to one, 'Go,' and he goes, and to another, 'Come,' and he comes, and to my <u>servant</u>, 'Do this,' and he does it.* ESV

There are important parallels between biblical slavery and a biblical discipleship connection:

- <u>*exclusive ownership*</u>: Ro 5:18-19; Eph 2:1-3; 1 Pet 1:18-19; Rev 5:9; Ro 6:14-18; 1 Cor 7:23; Titus 2:14; Gal 5:24; Col 4:1
- <u>*complete submission*</u>: 1 John 2:3; 1 Pet 1:2; Ro 12:1; 1 John 3:22; 1 Cor 6:20
- <u>*singular devotion*</u>: Mt 6:24; Ro 7:5-6, 6:11-18; 1 Thess 1:9; Heb 13:21; 2 Cor 5:9; Col 1;10; 1 Thess 4:1; Ro 14:18
- <u>*total dependence*</u>: Mt 6:31-33; 1 Tim 6:8; Php 4:19; 2 Cor 9:8, 12:9
- <u>*personal accountability*</u>: Ro 14:12; 2 Cor 5:10; 2 Tim 4:8

These five characteristics come very close to being identical to the relationship between a father and child. The New Testament reflects the perspective of commanding believers to submit to Christ completely – not just as hired servants or spiritual employees – but as those who belong to Him totally (like a slave or child). We are told to obey Him without question and follow Him without complaint. Jesus is our Master, a fact we acknowledge every time we call Him Lord. We are His slaves, called humbly and wholeheartedly to obey and honor Him. But we do this in the context of a loving personal relationship.

FAMILY CONNECTION

Lastly, the Bible often speaks of our relationship with God in terms of "family," being a child of God, or a son of God. The use of "family" terms clearly intends to describe the unique nature our relationship with the Divine. Our God is a God of relationships experienced in the context of "family." This family connection or relationship is confirmed by the following:

FAMILY:
John 8:35-36 *A slave is not a permanent member of the family, but a son is part of the family forever. 36 So if the Son sets you free, you are truly free.* (NLT)

CHILDREN:
John 1:12 *. . . he gave the right to become children of God.* ESV

SONS:
Ephesians 1:5 *God decided in advance to adopt us into his own family by bringing us to himself through Jesus Christ . . .* NLT

CO-HEIR:
Romans 8:17 *and if children, then heirs—heirs of God and fellow heirs with Christ, provided we suffer with him in order that we may also be glorified with him.* ESV (see also Gal 3:29, 4:7)

The family relationship is quite clear, even to the amazing promise that we are "heirs" with Christ (Ro 8:17)! Are you serious? The Bible even refers to calling God "Abba" (Daddy). Because we are part of the family of God we receive rewards: being in the Kingdom of God, receiving eternal life, overcoming the world, and victory over sin. All these benefits are related to being a child of God. But as family members, we also have family responsibilities. We are to honor Him, obey Him, love Him, love others, use His spiritual gifts, grow, and mature.

SUMMARY/CONCLUSION

Scripture describes Christians as disciples, followers, aliens and strangers of God, citizens of heaven, light to the world, heirs of

God, joint heirs with Christ, members of His body, sheep in his flock, ambassadors in His service, children, sons, family, friends, elect, and of all things, slaves.

Thus, we have a unique relationship with our God:

- we were slaves to sin; now we are slaves of Christ,
- we were sons of disobedience; now we are adopted sons of righteousness,
- we live in this world, but we are citizens of heaven, and
- we were foreigners and aliens, but now we are fellow citizens with God and His family.

With a relationship, however, comes responsibility. The Bible urges us to live lives worthy of God (1 Thessalonians 2:12). And, because we are receiving a kingdom that cannot be shaken, the Bible suggests that we be thankful, and worship God acceptably with reverence and awe (Hebrews 12:28).

We can therefore conclude that the Bible does require a personal relationship with God. It is unique and described in a number of different ways, but it is clear that a relationship is necessary. In fact, one might go so far as to say that it is the basic building-block of God's plan for His people. And like a family or a master-slave relationship, our connection to God must be exclusive. There can be no other God but Yahweh!

DISCUSSION QUESTIONS

1. In the real world (in your life) what gets in the way of having an intimate relationship with Christ?

2. What experiences in your life confirm that God desires a relationship with His people?

3. How do you feel about being a slave to Christ? Does that sit right with you?

4. Do you agree with our explanation of Mt 7:21-23 in the "KNOWING CHRIST" Section (page 23)? Why? Why not?

5. Jeremiah 9:23-24 instructs us not to boast except that we "understand" and know God. What do you think it means to "understand" Him?

Prayer: Lord, I don't care about how our relationship is described, just make it personal and growing so that You are always and constantly my guide, my anchor, and my God.

My Personal Prayer

What I Want to Remember

Enter some notes and information that you want to remember about this week's study. It might be a Scripture verse or two, something new you learned, something you want to do, something you want to change, or just something you want to be sure to remember.

Wisdom to Action
Challenge

In what practical way can you imitate God's love today, especially towards someone who may be difficult to love?

Lesson 3
Being Available to God

The life of a Jesus follower can be identified by a number of characteristics describing the nature of his relationship with God. These are not performance activities, but relationship characteristics. They are the stepping stones to establishing, building, and cementing an intimate love relationship with Jesus.

LESSON MEDITATION

Meditate on Hebrews 12:5-8 during your Quiet Time this week:

Hebrews 12:5-8 *And have you forgotten the exhortation that addresses you as sons? "My son, do not regard lightly the discipline of the Lord, nor be weary when reproved by him. 6 For the Lord disciplines the one he loves, and chastises every son whom he receives." 7 It is for discipline that you have to endure. God is treating you as sons. For what son is there whom his father does not discipline? 8 If you are left without discipline, in which all have participated, then you are illegitimate children and not sons.* ESV

Questions to think about:

1. What is God saying to you about this passage?
2. Have you ever felt "disciplined" because you did not make yourself available?
3. What positive things have you learned from God's discipline?
4. What is always the goal of God's correction?

INTRODUCTION

Being available in the biblical context means I am willing to do something or assume some responsibility for God or the Kingdom. This would mean I was ready, willing, and present. I will respond to the call of God. When God calls I react like Abraham and begin packing to leave.

Absolutely nothing is said about being qualified or having the necessary skills. God qualifies those He calls. It is nonsense to think that God would call someone to a task they could not do, He were not going to provide the necessary tools. God does not call people to failures.

We will cover three important concepts in this lesson.

First, we are being changed as a result of our salvation. The technical Christian term would be that we are being *sanctified*. Sanctification is the state or process of growing in divine grace (spiritual growth) as a result of a commitment to Christ.

Second, the Jesus follower makes himself available to God for spiritual growth and ministry during this time of sanctification. We need to recognize the work of Christ and the Holy Spirit in our lives and make ourselves ready and available for His calling on our life.

Third, there is nothing said or implied that being qualified, skilled, capable, or able is necessary. We are simply asked to say, "Yes."

NEW CREATION

Q1. What do we learn from the following verses?

2 Corinthians 5:17 *Therefore, if anyone is in Christ, he is a new creation. The old has passed away; behold, the new has come.* ESV [see also Eph 4:24; Col 3:10; Gal 6:15]

2 Corinthians 3:18 *And we all, with unveiled face, beholding the glory of the Lord, are being transformed into the same image from one degree of glory to another. . .* ESV

Romans 8:29 *For those whom he foreknew he also predestined to be conformed to the image of his Son, in order that he might be the firstborn among many brothers.* ESV

Q2. In your own words, what is God doing in the above Scriptures?

Obviously from the above passages there is a major overhaul going on in our lives once we have committed our lives to Jesus. And, it is significant! Colossians 3:10 also refers to this overhaul and describes it as "putting on a new self."

Paul describes it further in Romans 12:1-2 where he indicates that we renew our minds in order that we can understand the will of God. However you describe this process, it means fundamental change in our lives.

WE ARE BLESSED – ACT LIKE IT

Ephesians 1:3-14 and 2:4-10 tell us that Christ followers have been showered with blessing after blessing. Here's what is happening and what we should do about it:

1. Blessed with every spiritual blessing – so rejoice in it
2. Chosen by Him – so celebrate it
3. Holy and blameless – so live like it
4. Adopted as sons and daughters – so be proud of it
5. Redeemed – so delight in it
6. Forgiven – so be humble because of it
7. Guaranteed an inheritance – so look forward to it

8. Given the Holy Spirit – so use Him
9. Made alive (spiritually) – so embrace it
10. Seated with Christ – so walk in it
11. Saved by grace – so believe it
12. Created for good works – so do it

I am a child of God, loved by God, redeemed by God, and nothing will ever change that . . . *SO I SHOULD ACT LIKE IT!*

Q3. If we agree that all these benefits are true, what prevents us from making ourselves available? What causes us not to live and act like the person who has the most valuable gift ever given?

WALK WORTHY

The Bible urges us to walk worthy with our God. Therefore, we should act like it, take advantage of it, and live like it. Ephesians 4:1 states it very bluntly: *"I urge you to walk in a manner worthy of the calling to which you have been called."* (ESV) Being worthy of something means one deserves respect or honor, even praise. Our relationship should honor our God.

Q4. What does "living a life worthy of your calling" mean to you in the following verses:

Colossians 1:9-10 *And so, from the day we heard, we have not ceased to pray for you, asking that you may be filled with the knowledge of his will in all spiritual wisdom and understanding, 10 so as to walk in a manner worthy of the Lord, fully pleasing to him, bearing fruit in every good work and increasing in the knowledge of God.* ESV

Philippians 1:27 *Only let your manner of life be worthy of the gospel of Christ, so that whether I come and see you or am absent, I may hear of you that you are standing firm in one spirit, with one mind striving side by side for the faith of the gospel . . . ESV*

Observe that in Php 1:27 above the result is unity in the Body.

We can conclude that walking worthy means I am living a life that respects and honors God. My life has value. It is deserving of respect or praise and God is the power behind that life and He should get the glory. In other words (as Paul might say), we are "in Christ" so live a life that is worthy of that relationship.

Paul makes it very clear how God wants us to act when in Ephesians 5:1 he says that we are to be imitators of God. At first glance that seems like a tall order, at least for me. But the concept is that God want us to live upright and righteous lives that honor our Creator.

Q5. What do you think Paul is really talking about in Ephesians 5:1? Can we really imitate God?

We are being changed, we are being transformed, and we are being sanctified. A Christ follower's contribution to that process is to have a personal relationship with God and make himself available.

WILLING and AVAILABLE

Being available to God means that we are willing to be used by God or we are willing to work for the Kingdom when He calls us.

Note what you learn about being available in the following passages.

Psalms 51:12-13 *Restore to me the joy of your salvation, and uphold me with a willing spirit. 13 Then I will teach transgressors your ways, and sinners will return to you.* ESV

Isaiah 1:18-20 *"Come now, let us reason together, says the Lord: though your sins are like scarlet, they shall be as white as snow; though they are red like crimson, they shall become like wool. 19 If you are willing and obedient, you shall eat the good of the land; 20 but if you refuse and rebel, you shall be eaten by the sword; for the mouth of the Lord has spoken."* ESV

Mark 14:38 ESV *Watch and pray that you may not enter into temptation. The spirit indeed is willing, but the flesh is weak.*

1 Peter 5:2-3 *. . . the shepherd the flock of God that is among you, exercising oversight, not under compulsion, but willingly, as God would have you; not for shameful gain, but eagerly; 3 not domineering over those in your charge, but being examples to the flock.* ESV

Q6. How might you summarize what you learned above about being willing and available?

Being willing means I do not refuse to do something. I am ready to do something when called upon. I am simply ready, willing, and able to help.

It may mean I have thought about or considered the question and decided I will do something. David asks God to give him a willing spirit but in Mark 14:38 we see the spirit is willing but the body (flesh) is weak. Isaiah indicates above that being willing can overcome a lot of sin in my life.

ABRAM (Abraham) WAS AVAILABLE

Genesis 12:1-5 *Now the Lord said to Abram, "Go from your country and your kindred and your father's house to the land that I will show you. . . . 4 So Abram went, as the Lord had told him, and Lot went with him. Abram was seventy-five years old when he departed from Haran. . . . and they set out to go to the land of Canaan.* ESV

Q7. What do you learn from the above passage about how Abraham responded to God?

What can you conclude from Abraham's decisions and actions in Genesis 22 when he obeyed God and took his son Isaac away to be sacrificed? Did Abraham do anything that might confirm whether this was simply a heart responding in obedience or simply a desire for adventure? Did it represent the character of Abraham's relationship with God? If so, what is it?

Abraham certainly demonstrated trust and confidence in God. For Abraham to do this he had to have had a <u>deep personal trust and faith relationship</u> with God. A real <u>heart</u> relationship! Clearly Abraham had to have believed he was talking to God – and you can only believe it's God if you have talked with Him before. There was a relationship.

Q8. What are some examples from Scripture where a Biblical character like Abraham made themselves available for God?

1. Who went to Egypt with a little one?_____

2. Who gave up boats and sea food?_____

3. Who was told to go and pray for Saul of Tarsus?_____

4. Who climbed a tree?_____

5. Who said, "Here I am; send me?"_____

6. Who went through fire for God? _____

7. Who decided not to run from God on His second request?

_____

8. Who married a prostitute at God's request? _____

SEEKING CLARIFICATION

It's not unreasonable to make sure you understand what God is telling you. Asking God, "Did I hear that right?" may be necessary. For example in Acts 9:13-16 Ananias asked:

> *"Lord, I have heard from many about this man, how much evil he has done to your saints at Jerusalem. 14 And here he has authority from the chief priests to bind all who call on your name." 15 But the Lord said to him, "Go, for he is a chosen instrument of mine to carry my name before the Gentiles and kings and the children of Israel. 16 For I will show him how much he must suffer for the sake of my name."* ESV

Throughout history some have refused God's calling on their lives. Other than Jonah, can you think of anyone else who ran from God, deliberately disobeyed God, or refused God's calling? I can think of several: (1) Adam and Eve, (2) Cain, (3) Israel continually turned to other gods, and (4) Peter denied Jesus at the cross. Can you think of others?

CONCLUSION

The Christian life involves learning to live out here on earth what is already true before God: we are blessed, chosen, holy, adopted, redeemed, forgiven, made alive, and created for good works. Nothing that we do can take away from these blessings. They are finished works. We should live like who we are in Christ. We are forgiven . . . we should live like it. We are holy and blameless . . . believe it. We are sons and daughters of the King . . . rejoice in it. We have access to the Father . . . use it.

Practically speaking, Christ-like character and conduct must be developed. God will not leave us the way we are – we are being trained, led, taught, and disciplined by God on a continual basis to be transformed into the image of Christ.

THOUGHT QUESTIONS

1. Given all you have read and studied, what is most likely to motivate you to be available to God's calling in your life?

2. In the real world (in your life) what gets in the way of making yourself available to God? What makes success difficult or elusive?

3. In <u>your</u> opinion what are the three most important characteristics of a person who successfully makes himself available to God?

4. Was there ever a time in the past when you were more available? What were the circumstances? What changed?

5. What is the <u>key</u> ingredient for <u>you</u> to be available?

Prayer: Lord, help me to be ready and willing when you call. Allow all I do to bring praise to Your Holy Name.

My Personal Prayer

What I Want to Remember

Enter some notes and information that you want to remember about this week's study. It might be a Scripture verse or two, something new you learned, something you want to do, something you want to change, or just something you want to be sure to remember.

Wisdom to Action
Challenge

What area of your life are you holding back from God? How can you make yourself more available to His call this week, despite any perceived inadequacies?

Lesson 4
Pursuing and Seeking God

The life of a Jesus follower can be identified by a number of characteristics describing the nature of his relationship with God. These are not performance activities, but relationship characteristics. They are the stepping stones to establishing, building, and cementing an intimate love relationship with Jesus.

LESSON MEDITATION

Meditate on Psalm 34 during your Quiet Time this week. Verses 1-14 define the actions of the righteous and 15-22 tell us how the Lord responds. Look closely at the verbs in 1-14 and consider if they are describing one who seeks God.

Verbs: extol; praise; boast; glorify; exalt; sought; looked; called; fear; taste; fear; come; keep; turn.

DEFINITIONS

This lesson will focus on how a Jesus follower seeks after or pursues God. This is the process of searching for and acquiring intimacy with God. The purpose of such pursuit is a relationship with God or heart knowledge about God.

The Greek translation of the words translated "seek" implies a searching activity <u>associated with worship</u>. In Hebrews 11:6 we are instructed to "diligently seek," adding some importance to the process. The Old Testament Hebrew implies to search out and strive after something – particularly God. Such searching is meant to uncover knowledge through diligent and maybe even difficult investigation.

Generally we can conclude that seeking or pursuing requires intentional action and purpose! We need to be active, not passive. We certainly cannot expect to find God, experience God, or enjoy God, if we are not seeking Him.

Q1. How would you evaluate your personal ability or commitment to seek after God? Good? Bad? So-so?

OBSERVATIONS

What can we learn about seeking in the following verses?

Acts 17:27 *. . . that they should seek God, in the hope that they might feel their way toward him and find him. Yet he is actually not far from each one of us . . .* ESV [see also 1 Chron 28:9]

1 Chronicles 22:19 *Now set your mind and heart to seek the Lord your God. . . .* ESV

Zephaniah 2:3 *Seek the Lord, all you humble of the land, who do his just commands; seek righteousness; seek humility; perhaps you may be hidden on the day of the anger of the Lord.* ESV

Q2. Based on Ps 24:5, what is received by those who seek?
Psalms 24:3-6 *Who shall ascend the hill of the Lord? And who shall stand in his holy place? 4 He who has clean hands and a pure heart, who does not lift up his soul to what is false and does not swear deceitfully. 5 He will receive blessing from the Lord and righteousness from the God of his salvation. 6 Such is the generation of those who seek him, who seek the face of the God of Jacob.* Selah ESV

Q3. The above passage has a requirement. What is it?

Q4. Which verse or verses above are the most difficult or challenging for you? Why?

God can be found! The pursuing simply needs to be intentional, active, and sometimes aggressive. We must be earnestly seeking God. There are benefits such as: (1) finding Him, (2) being sheltered, and (3) receive blessing and vindication.

Q5. What do we learn from the following passage about pursuing?
Psalms 63:1 *O God, you are my God; earnestly I seek you; my soul thirsts for you; my flesh faints for you, as in a dry and weary land where there is no water.* ESV

Q6. In Ps 63:1 above describe how we are to go about seeking. What is the nature of the process?

BENEFITS OF SEEKING GOD

Q7. What benefits can you identify in the following verses?

2 Chronicles 26:3-5 *Uzziah . . . did what was right in the eyes of the LORD . . . He sought God during the days of Zechariah, who instructed him in the fear of God. As long as he sought the LORD, God gave him success.* ESV

Psalms 9:10 *. . . for you, O Lord, have not forsaken those who seek you.* ESV

Psalms 34:4 *I sought the LORD, and he answered me and delivered me from all my fears.* ESV

Psalms 34:10 *. . . those who seek the LORD lack no good thing.* ESV

Proverbs 28:5 *Evil men do not understand justice, but those who seek the LORD understand it completely.* ESV

Q8. Have you ever experienced any of the benefits above? If so, note below or share your experience.

Q9. Are the benefits in Psalm 34 enough to motivate you personally to pursue God? Why? Why not? If not, what would it take?

HOW TO SEEK GOD

On the surface, "seeking" may sound like a simple process, but in reality it may not be as easy as it may sound. As indicated above, some form of intentional action is required. What type of action? What and how should we go about seeking? What does it really mean to seek God or seek His face? Scripture has a great deal to say about how we should seek God. Note in the space provided what you learn in Isa 55 about seeking:

Isaiah 55:6 *Seek the Lord while he may be found; call upon him while he is near . . .* ESV

We need to do it urgently, immediately, with pressing importance, or desperately. Here there is a hint that we must do it now, because there may be a time when we either cannot seek him or that it may not be possible to find Him. Thus, we should not delay when we have opportunities. We cannot assume we can do this at another stage in life – that time may never come. The time is <u>now</u>! Time is of the essence.

Psalm 105:4 *Seek the Lord and his strength; seek his presence continually!* ESV

Q10. What does it mean to seek his presence "continually" based on the following scriptures?

Matthew 6:33 *But seek first the kingdom of God and his righteousness, and all these things will be added to you.* ESV

Jeremiah 29:12-13 *Then you will call upon me and come and pray to me, and I will hear you. 13 You will seek me and find me. When you seek me with all your heart . . .* ESV
[see also Dt 4:29 and Ps 119:58]

>We can conclude that seeking God with all our heart should be a serious and earnest undertaking. It should not be done lightly as if the outcome is of little importance. We should seek, serve, and love God with a committed intensity. This means we have a close personal and intimate relationship. It is not just a mind seeking information, but a heart that finds and connects with its Creator, Savior, and King!

Hebrews 11:6 *And it is impossible to please God without faith. Anyone who wants to come to him must believe that God exists and that he rewards those who sincerely {earnestly} seek him.* NLT (see also Ps 63:1)

Seeking sincerely or earnestly means we are diligently undertaking to find God or His presence in our life. It is an intense and serious undertaking. This might also be described with the words fervently, whole-heartedly, or gravely. A good example is Elijah who prayed earnestly:

James 5:17-18 *Elijah was a man with a nature like ours, and he prayed fervently that it might not rain, and for three years and six months it did not rain on the earth. 18 Then he prayed again, and heaven gave rain, and the earth bore its fruit.* ESV

Q11. Identify and define the "how" in the following verse.
2 Chronicles 15:15 *And all Judah rejoiced over the oath, for they had sworn with all their heart and had sought him with their whole desire [eagerly], and he was found by them, and the Lord gave them rest all around.* ESV

Q12. This verse also indicates there is a benefit to seeking. What is it and what does it mean?

Psalms 77:2 *In the day of my trouble I seek the Lord; in the night my hand is stretched out without wearying; my soul refuses to be comforted.* ESV

Psalms 40:16 *But may all who seek you rejoice and be glad in you; may those who love your salvation say continually, "Great is the Lord!"* ESV (also Ps 22:26; 70:4)

Praise and worship should accompany our seeking. What we do and how we go about it should exalt God. We should not become frustrated or anxious. *God's plan may be that the process is long so that the finding is sweet.* God does not say that when we start seeking we will immediately find – the promise is just that we <u>will</u> find. So, while we are seeking we should do it with praise and an attitude of gratitude.

One approach for some believers in seeking the face of God is to practice spiritual disciplines. A spiritual discipline is an act or behavior which is deliberately chosen and intentionally practiced in order to focus on God and grow in obedience in the Christian life. Therefore one might engage in the following:

- Study and Meditation
- Community and Submission
- Service and Secrecy
- Solitude and Silence
- Reflection and Confession
- Worship and Celebration
- Simplicity and Fasting
- Prayer and Listening

HINDRANCES

In the real world (in your life) what gets in the way of pursuing God? What makes success difficult or elusive?

1. What are the distractions that you battle in pursuing God?

2. What would lessen the distractions or make them go away for <u>you</u>?

THOUGHT OR DISCUSSION QUESTIONS

1. What do you believe are the three most important characteristics of a person who successfully pursues God?

a. _____

b. _____

c. _____

2. To what degree are you currently pursuing God? How would you evaluate your status after studying this lesson?

3. What is the key ingredient for <u>you</u> in making this happen in <u>your</u> life?

CONCLUSION

It is reasonable to suggest that in some way our seeking, striving, and searching are all part of our Christian walk. If we have true saving faith, then to some degree we have found Christ, but our knowledge of Him or our relationship with Him will not necessarily be complete, full, or effective. Thus, we need to continually seek and pursue Him so that we can delight ourselves in a growing relationship with the Almighty.

For me it is an attempt to know Him on a level where I perceive His will for my life. And, for me that is not always easy. It is my hope to walk in obedience and my seeking is purposed to align my actions with His will for my life. For you it will most likely be different. Each of us relates to the Godhead in different ways. But whatever and however we seek to know God, we must do it with all our hearts. Relentlessly!

Prayer: Lord, give me the strength, courage, and will to pursue You _relentlessly_, all the days of my life!

My Personal Prayer

What I Want to Remember

Enter some notes and information that you want to remember about this week's study. It might be a Scripture verse or two, something new you learned, something you want to do, something you want to change, or just something you want to be sure to remember.

Wisdom to Action
Challenge

What intentional step can you take this week to actively seek God more earnestly in your daily routine?

Lesson 5
Abiding in God

The life of a Jesus follower can be identified by a number of characteristics describing the nature of his relationship with God. These are not performance activities, but relationship characteristics. They are the stepping stones to establishing, building, and cementing an intimate love relationship with Jesus.

LESSON MEDITATION

Meditate on Eph 3:16-19 during your Quiet Time this week.

Ephesians 3:16-19 . . . *that according to the riches of his glory he may grant you to be strengthened with <u>power</u> through his Spirit in your inner being, 17 so that Christ may dwell in your hearts through faith – that you, being rooted and grounded in love, 18 may have <u>strength</u> to comprehend with all the saints what is the breadth and length and height and depth, 19 and to know the love of Christ that surpasses knowledge, that you may be <u>filled</u> with all the fullness of God.* ESV

THE SCENE (John 15)

One can imagine Jesus touching the vines and branches. Dew may have formed on the branches and leaves. Jesus' fingers pause where the massive trunk (or the vine) divides into the branches. *"Abide in Me, and I in you,"* He says. Then He directs the disciples' attention down the branch – which is already showing signs of fruit . . . *"As the branch cannot bear fruit of itself, unless it abides in the vine, neither can you, unless you abide in Me."*

Do the disciples understand what Jesus is saying? Are they even paying attention? Then He says: *". . . He who abides in Me, and I in him, bears <u>much fruit</u>; for without Me you can do nothing."*

At this critical point Jesus is describing the most important part of His message. Abiding! He says," I want you to have a close, constant, intimate relationship with Me." Abiding is the activity that will ultimately produce the fruit because the power comes from abiding. I don't just decide I am going to obey and go out and knock the world dead with my witness and service. Rather, after I know Christ and have a deep relationship, then, through His power I produce fruit.

The branch with the largest, least-obstructed connection with the vine is abiding the most and will have the greatest potential for producing a large crop. And that is what Jesus is saying through the use of this metaphor about the vine:

- abide in Me,
- stay closely connected, and
- allow Me to provide the power and strength.

Jesus is showing the disciples how an ongoing, vital connection with Him will directly impact the amount of His power at work in their lives. In six verses John says "abide" ten times. We should sense the passion, drama, and poignancy of what He is saying and how critically important is the message!

Jesus knows that He is going to the Cross and is about to leave His friends, yet, His focus on that night was telling His disciples that "*we must remain together.*" You must "*abide in Me and I in you.*" He knows that in the coming years, these men will be called on to produce an unheard-of amount of fruit – enough to turn the whole world upside down. And the one thing, <u>the most important thing</u> they need to do, is remain in Him – to abide.[3]

> *Abide in me, and I in you. As the branch cannot*
> *bear fruit by itself, unless it abides in the vine,*
> *neither can you, unless you abide in me.*
> *I am the vine; you are the branches. Whoever abides*
> *in me and I in him, he it is that bears much fruit,*
> *for apart from me you can do nothing.*
> John 15:4-5 ESV

Remember the implication is that we are helpless to bear <u>much</u> fruit alone. He says . . . *"for without Me you can do nothing"* (15:5). Abiding doesn't measure how much you know about your faith or your Bible, it describes the relationship between you and Jesus, because you:

- seek after,
- long for,
- thirst after,
- wait for,
- see,
- know,
- love,
- hear, and
- respond to . . . the Christ, the Son of God.

How do you react to this scene? Does this resonate? Can you imagine the scene? Read the description of this scene again and put yourself in the midst of the disciples while Jesus is talking.

Record your thoughts:

The challenge in abiding is to break through the dutiful activities, the religious rules, the external expectations of others, to knowing God through a personal relationship with Jesus – the True Vine. Again and again Jesus withdrew to a solitary or private place to meet with God. He was <u>always</u> aware of the need for His Father's abiding presence. So it must be with us. We must keep in contact with Jesus and it must be intentional:

- We must set aside time to pray.
- We must set aside time for His Word.
- We must intentionally set aside time for Him.

CAUTION: "Abiding" is not an end in itself. The point is that abiding results in demonstrating love, obedience to Jesus' teachings, bearing fruit – the fruit of the Vine! The life flows through the branches from the Vine. It is the power and presence of Jesus being active in our lives. It is not me but Him! So if I want to live the life of a Jesus follower, I must stay close to the source of divine power – Christ!

HOW DO WE ABIDE?

Scripture indicates some "requirements" for abiding in Christ. In 1 John we find four important characteristics about people who abide. The Gospel of John confirms all this in one passage. Note in the space provided what you learn about how to abide:

1 John 2:9 *Whoever says he is in the light and hates his brother is still in darkness.* ESV

1 John 4:12 *. . . if we love one another, God abides in us and his love is perfected in us.* ESV

1 John 4:16 *. . . whoever abides in love abides in God, and God abides in him.* ESV

John 15:9-10 *As the Father has loved me, so have I loved you. Abide in my love. 10 If you keep my commandments, you will abide in my love, just as I have kept my Father's commandments and abide in his love.* ESV

Q1. How would you summarize these instructions?

In the New Testament abiding means to maintain an unbroken fellowship, be constantly present with someone, or to put forth constant influence upon someone. In the phraseology used by John, God is said to abide or remain in Christ. He is continually operative in Him by His divine influence, energy, and presence (John 14:10).[4]

Jesus said, "Abide in Me." Thus, abiding in Christ means:

- I am in a constant relationship,
- I am in a life-sustaining union or association,
- I am living in conformity with His teachings, and
- I am "in Christ" or living in the Spirit (Paul).

Q2. Is that how you think about abiding? Do you agree? Or, do you view it in some other way?

Q3. What important concept(s) do you personally take away from the above?

Q4. What do you think is the <u>essential</u> ingredient (requirement) in abiding?

SPEND TIME WITH GOD

Jesus wants us to be "with Him" (Mk 3:14). Thus, *time is required*. Time spent with Jesus by reading or studying the Bible, talking or praying to Him is not just a priority, it is *absolutely essential* in abiding. If an intimate relationship is not developing, nothing else will be right. So abide! Regardless of the nature of the activity (ministry, good works, or fruit of the Spirit), the key is abiding (being connected), holding on tightly to the Vine. Our Christian life is characterized first and foremost by a relationship that requires spending time with our Lord. Any good works (fruit) will flow from that relationship, because it is the relationship with Him that produces the performance.

> **John 15:5** *I am the vine; you are the branches. Whoever abides in me and I in him, he it is that bears much fruit, for apart from me you can do nothing.* ESV

APART FROM ME

John 15:4-6 *Abide in me, and I in you . . . unless you abide in me . . . apart from me you can do nothing. If anyone does not abide in me he is thrown away like a branch and withers . . .* ESV

Q5. What is the most important part of the above passage?

HOW TO LOVE

John 15:4, 9, 12, 17 *Abide in me, and I in you. As the branch cannot bear fruit by itself, unless it abides in the vine, neither can you, unless you abide in me . . . 9 As the Father has loved me, so have I loved you. Abide in my love . . . 12 "This is my commandment, that you love one another as I have loved you . . . 17 These things I command you, so that you will love one another.* ESV

Q6. What are the three commands in the above passage:

1.

2.

3.

Q7. How does the above say we are to love each other, and what does it mean?

In this passage love and obedience are <u>not</u> defined by a list of requirements but rather by the example of Jesus. Record below how Jesus tells us to love and obey?

> **LOVE: John 15:12** *. . . love one another as I have loved you.* ESV

> **OBEY: John 15:10** *If you keep my commandments, you will abide in my love, just as I have kept my Father's commandments and abide in his love.* ESV

Q8. Now apply that concept to your life. What does that mean for you personally?

CONFIRMATION OF ABIDING

How do we know if we are abiding? 1 John 2:5-6 says, "*but whoever keeps his word, in him truly the love of God is perfected. By this we may be sure that we are in him: 6 whoever says he abides in him ought to walk in the same way in which he walked.*" (ESV) Thus, we are to obey and walk (live) as He did.

Q9. In your opinion what is the key to following the instruction above (abiding)?

WALKING IN THE SPIRIT (Romans 8:1-17)

The first 17 verses of Romans 8 indicate Paul's views regarding living life in the Spirit, or the nature of being "in Christ." These verses compare life in the Spirit with living according to our sinful nature. It's a battle! Read these verses and indicate below the primary thought in the following verses:

8:1

8:2

8:9

8:17

Let's examine Romans 8:5-8 more closely:

Romans 8:5-8 *For those who live according to the flesh set their <u>minds</u> on the things of the flesh, but those who live according to the Spirit set their <u>minds</u> on the things of the Spirit. 6 To set the <u>mind</u> on the flesh is death, but to set the <u>mind</u> on the Spirit is life and peace. 7 For the <u>mind</u> that is set on the flesh is hostile to God, for it does not submit to God's law; indeed, it cannot. 8 Those who are in the flesh cannot please God.* ESV

Obviously since we underlined the word "mind" in the above passage we consider it a key to the meaning of the passage. Notice what Paul tells us in Romans 12:2 about the mind.

> *Do not be conformed to this world, but be transformed by the renewal of your <u>mind</u>, that by testing you may discern what is the will of God, what is good and acceptable and perfect.* (Romans 12:2 ESV)

Two perspectives are described here: that of the sinful nature and that of the Spirit. Therefore, set your mind on what the Spirit desires.

Q10. Look up the following Scriptures and record God's instructions concerning your thoughts and mind:

Hebrews 3:1

Philippians 4:8

Romans 12:3

Ephesians 4:23

1 Peter 1:13

Q11. Why do you think there is such a significant focus on the "mind"?

HINDRANCES

In the real world (in your life) what gets in the way of abiding in Christ? What makes success difficult or elusive? There are many distractions that can cloud our sight and our judgment.

1. What are the hindrances or distractions that <u>you</u> battle in <u>spending time</u> with God:

2. What would lessen your distractions or make them go away?

In summary, what is our responsibility? How do you personally think these concepts should impact your life? Our responsibility is to abide so that God can work through us. Otherwise nothing significant is likely to happen. Our aim must be to bring our heart, mind, and soul into the realization that Jesus is Lord!

THOUGHT QUESTIONS

1. Was there a time in the past when you were relatively successful in spending time with God? What were the circumstances? Why were you successful? What changed?

2. How would abiding look in <u>your</u> life? List the best three things (most important for you) that you would do to abide in Christ.

3. What is the key ingredient for <u>you</u> in making this happen in <u>your</u> life?

CONCLUSION

Let's face it, we have some responsibility here. In Mark 3:13-14 it is clear Jesus wants to spend time with us. It describes Jesus going up a mountainside and calling those He wanted with Him. He appointed twelve apostles (*that they might be with Him*) and that He might send them out to minister. It is obvious in the story of Martha and Mary that although serving is important, the most important activity is abiding (Luke 10:42).

If you are having a daily quiet time then you have jumped the biggest hurdle – spending time. You need a daily time with God in prayer, Bible study, meditation, and worship. Without this time you will never experience the full power of Christ in your life. He wants to spend time with you and you must make a firm commitment to spend time with Him. It's like making a commitment to be in church every Sunday morning.

Abiding in Christ is an absolute requirement for living a Christian life – it produces an intimate relationship with God. If you do not spend time with Him, being obedient to His teaching will be very difficult to accomplish. It is the relationship that produces fruit like obedience, humility, goodness, etc.

If you worry that your obedience and service are not what you want or what you think God wants, stop worrying and start abiding. Stop all the forced activity you think you are supposed to do and just spend time with Christ and let Him tell you and enable you to walk in His ways. Trying to do it in your own power simply will not work.

Prayer: Lord, enable me to abide in You.

My Personal Prayer

What I Want to Remember

Enter some notes and information that you want to remember about this week's study. It might be a Scripture verse or two, something new you learned, something you want to do, something you want to change, or just something you want to be sure to remember.

Wisdom to Action
Challange

How can you more consciously abide in Christ today? Identify one way to stay connected to Him throughout your day.

Lesson 6
Knowing God

The life of a Jesus follower can be identified by a number of characteristics describing the nature of his relationship with God. These are not performance activities, but relationship characteristics. They are the stepping stones to establishing, building, and cementing an intimate love relationship with Jesus.

LESSON MEDITATION

Meditate on the following during your Quiet Time this week.

2 Thessalonians 1:5-9 *<u>This</u> is evidence of the righteous judgment of God, that you may be considered worthy of the kingdom of God, for which you are also suffering— 6 since indeed God considers it just to repay with affliction those who afflict you, 7 and to grant relief to you who are afflicted as well as to us, when the Lord Jesus is revealed from heaven with his mighty angels 8 in flaming fire, inflicting vengeance on those who do not know God and on those who do not obey the gospel of our Lord Jesus. 9 They will suffer the punishment of eternal destruction, away from the presence of the Lord and from the glory of his might . . . ESV*

KNOWING GOD

What does it mean to "know" God? This question is not asking if we know *about* God, but do we know Him like we know our best friend. Biblically, to know God initially means we have a saving relationship with Jesus. We have been reconciled to God through Christ and are saved. Reconciliation means that there is harmony between God and man and the relationship that was destroyed by sin has been restored.

> **Romans 5:11** *More than that, we also rejoice in God through our Lord Jesus Christ, through whom we have now received reconciliation.* ESV

The knowing God we are discussing in this lesson means there is fellowship or a relationship. Paul refers to "knowing" in Philippians:

> **Philippians 3:10-11** *that I may know him and the power of his resurrection, and may share his sufferings, becoming like him in his death, 11 that by any means possible I may attain the resurrection from the dead.* ESV

To know God more intimately may be the greatest pursuit in life. He wants us to know Him through a relationship. He wants intimate encounters with us. We can experience God through Scripture, prayer, events, and circumstances. We often experience Him most during difficult times and especially when we choose to put our trust in Him.

You might wonder why "knowing" could be so important. Habakkuk 2:14 says, "*For the earth will be filled with the knowledge of the glory of the Lord, as the waters cover the sea.*" (NIV) That certainly raises knowledge and understanding to a new level. But it is Hosea who drives the knowledge of God to a higher level: "*My people are destroyed for lack of knowledge. Because you have rejected knowledge, I will reject you from serving as My priest. Since you have forgotten the law of your God, I will also forget your sons.*" (Hosea 4:6 HCSB)

To "know" Him ultimately means we have an intimate relationship with Him that has developed over time.

A JESUS FOLLOWER KNOWS GOD

What do we learn or observe in the following?

1 John 5:20 *And we know that the Son of God has come and has given us understanding, so that we may know him who is true.* ESV

1 John 4:8 *Anyone who does not love does not know God, because God is love.* ESV

John 17:3 *And this is eternal life, that they know you the only true God, and Jesus Christ whom you have sent.* ESV

2 Peter 1:3 *His divine power has granted to us all things that pertain to life and godliness, through the knowledge of him who called us to his own glory and excellence,* ESV

Q1. Why does Paul suggest in the following that we should press on?
Philippians 3:10-12 *. . . that I may know him and the power of his resurrection, and may share his sufferings, becoming like him in his death, . . . , but I press on to make it my own, because Christ Jesus has made me his own.* ESV

Q2. Based on the following, how do we know that we know Him?

John 14:17 ... *even the Spirit of truth, whom the world cannot receive, because it neither sees him nor knows him. You know him, for he dwells with you and will be in you.* ESV

Q3. If you had to choose, which of the seven passages above do you think is the most important? Why?

OBSERVATIONS FROM 1 JOHN

What do we learn from the following verses about knowing Christ?

1 John 2:3 *And by this we know that we have come to know him, if we keep his commandments.* ESV

1 John 2:6 *whoever says he abides in him ought to walk in the same way in which he walked.* ESV

1 John 4:21 *And this commandment we have from him: whoever loves God must also love his brother.* ESV

Thus, knowing God means we live in obedience, love God, and love one another. We are to walk as Jesus walked and obey His teachings.

Q4. Based on 1 John 2:3 and 2:6 above, how would one prove he knew God, or had knowledge of God?

The Greeks claimed to know God intellectually and viewed it as an intellectual exercise to know about God. But there was no feeling or ethical obligation associated with that knowing. John is trying to make the point that we show we know God by our obedience to His ways and to Christ because we follow His commands and teachings.

For the committed follower, the privilege or grace received through Christ brings an associated obligation. It matters not how much effort we may have expended or invested the result must still be produced by an obedient moral action.

JEREMIAH KNEW GOD

Jeremiah 9:23-24 *Thus says the Lord: "Let not the wise man boast in his wisdom, let not the mighty man boast in his might, let not the rich man boast in his riches, 24 but let him who boasts boast in this, that he understands and knows me, that I am the Lord who practices steadfast love, justice, and righteousness in the earth. For in these things I delight, declares the Lord."* ESV

Q5. What do you learn from the above passage about knowing God?

Q6. Why do you think Jeremiah specified that we should "understand" the Lord in conjunction with knowing?

GOING DEEPER ON KNOWING GOD

Titus 1:16 *They profess to know God, but they deny him by their works. They are detestable, disobedient, unfit for any good work.* ESV

1 John 4:8 *Anyone who does not love does not know God, because God is love.* ESV

1 John 3:6 *No one who abides in him keeps on sinning; no one who keeps on sinning has either seen him or known him.* ESV

Jeremiah 22:16 *He judged the cause of the poor and needy; then it was well. Is not this to know me declares the Lord.* ESV

Q7. List the requirements for knowing God in each of the verses above:

Titus 1:16

1 Jn 4:8

1 Jn 3:6

Jer 22:16

Q8. What can you conclude from this summary?

GOD WANTS TO KNOW YOU

Matthew 7:21-23 *Not everyone who says to me, 'Lord, Lord,' will enter the kingdom of heaven, but the one who does the will of my Father who is in heaven. 22 On that day many will say to me, 'Lord, Lord, did we not prophesy in your name, and cast out demons in your name, and do many mighty works in your name?' 23 And then will I declare to them, <u>'I never knew you</u>; depart from me, you workers of lawlessness.'* ESV

We show our true self and the sincerity of our words through our actions. Rest assured that great words do not replace intentional good deeds in the family of God. The one proof stated over and over again in Scripture is that obedience demonstrates our heart. If you say you love someone and then do things that are hurtful or rebellious, the only conclusion is you don't really love them?

> **Faith without obedience is a contradiction and love without obedience is an impossibility!**

Q9. What is the meaning or implication in Mt 7:21-23 that makes *not being known by God* catastrophic?

Q10. What are the hindrances or distractions that you battle in understanding and knowing God?

SUMMARY/CONCLUSION

In the Old Testament, knowing God was more a matter of knowing the character of God. God revealed Himself to His people through experience, often resulting in the names used to identify Him. Through His names Israel learned the true character of God. For example:

Three Major Names	Meaning
1. God *Elohim*	powerful
2. LORD *I AM (Yahweh)*	covenant God ("Jehovah")
3. Lord *Adonai*	master

Other Names	
4. *El Elyon*	most high
5. *El Shaddai*	almighty
6. *Jehovah Jireh*	provides
7. *Jehovah Rophe*	heals
8. *Jehovah Nissi*	my banner
9. *Jehovah Mekadesh*	sanctifies
10. *Jehovah Shalom*	peace
11. *Jehovah Tsidkenu*	righteousness
12. *Jehovah Rohi*	shepherd

In the New Testament knowing God centers around having a right relationship with Him. If that exists we obey His teaching and walk as He did. In doing this we develop a relationship with Him that will motivate us to live in obedience and serve others.

Paul might describe this relationship as being "in Christ" or living "in the spirit." John described it as "abiding." Both describe the process or condition of knowing Christ and as that condition matures, it becomes an intimate love relationship. For some this process may occur relatively quickly and for others it may take longer.

Jeremiah confirms that our priority should be focused on God because if we are going to boast about anything in our life it ought to be about knowing Him – not about our jobs, our home, our family, or our church.

Q11. What would knowing God look like in <u>your</u> life? List the two most important things (most important for you) that you should do to know God on a more intimate basis.

PRAYER

Lord, help me to know the joy and intimacy of fellowship with You. I desire the peace that comes from knowing You. Give me an urgency and commitment in seeking and knowing You. Your Word says that we will come to know you if we are obedient to your commands. Lord, give me the ability to walk in Your ways. Bless me with understanding and knowledge of Your ways. Your Word says that the pure in heart are blessed and they will see God! Lord Jesus, give me the ability to be pure in heart so that I can see and know You.

My Personal Prayer

What I Want to Remember

Enter some notes and information that you want to remember about this week's study. It might be a Scripture verse or two, something new you learned, something you want to do, something you want to change, or just something you want to be sure to remember.

Wisdom to Action
Challenge

What aspect of God's character do you want to know more deeply? How can you actively pursue this knowledge in the coming week?

BONUS: Chapter 23 of A. W. Tozer's *The Knowledge of the Holy*

Do you want to bring back revival? Do you want to see the glory of God in our midst? Then, "Acquaint thyself with God!" We need a new transforming vision of God – the one that is the Majesty of the heavens, God the Lord Almighty, Maker of heaven and earth. We need to reacquaint ourselves with the one that sits upon the circle of the earth, who stretches out the heavens like a curtain and spreads them out as a tent to dwell in, who brings out His starry host by number and calls them by name, and who sees the works of man as vanity, yet extends His grace as a free gift to those men and women of faith.

The knowledge of God is freely given to those who desire to know Him. As the sunlight falls freely on the earth so does the knowledge of a holy God as a free gift to those who are open to receive it. But, this knowledge is difficult for most because there are conditions, and sinful man does not take kindly to conditions. Such conditions include:

- We must forsake sin!
- There must be a complete faith commitment of the whole life to Christ.
- There must be an understanding that we have died to sin and live to God through Christ Jesus.
- We must boldly reject the human values of the sinful world and separate ourselves from those things that unbelieving man worships.
- We must practice the art of long and loving meditation on the greatness of God.
- We must be in ministry and service to others, particularly to those in need.
- We must share our knowledge of God with others.
- Our life should be centered around our holy God.
- We should extol His greatness, faithfully representing our Savior in this world.

Lesson 7
Loving God

The life of a Jesus follower can be identified by a number of characteristics describing the nature of his relationship with God. These are not performance activities, but relationship characteristics. They are the stepping stones to establishing, building, and cementing an intimate love relationship with Jesus.

LESSON MEDITATION

Meditate on the following during your Quiet Time this week.

Romans 8:38-39 *For I am sure that neither death nor life, nor angels nor rulers, nor things present nor things to come, nor powers, 39 nor height nor depth, nor anything else in all creation, will be able to separate us from the love of God in Christ Jesus our Lord.* ESV

INTRODUCTION

One of the major objectives this week is to learn and understand what it really means to love God. Therefore, as you go through this week's lesson, when you find a possible or partial answer to that question, write down your finding or conclusion in the space under the "SUMMARY: LOVING GOD" section toward the end of this lesson.

Webster says that love is:

- strong affection for another arising out of kinship or personal ties,

- affection based on admiration, benevolence, or common interests,

- warm attachment, enthusiasm, or devotion,

- unselfish loyal and benevolent concern for the good of another (agape), and

- a person's adoration of God.

AGAPE

We want to focus on biblical agape love which is a "brotherly" love that is unconditional, humble, and selfless. Agape gives even if nothing is received in turn. It puts another's wants and needs above self. Agape will undergo hardship, sacrifice, or suffering for another's benefit. Agape love is a decision, not an emotion!

Love is the core of a Jesus follower – a love relationship with God. Everything in our life is dependent on the quality, depth, and nature of that relationship. Jesus set the standard when He said, "You shall love the Lord your God with all your heart and with all your soul and with all your mind." (Mt 22:37 ESV) This appears to be more than a mere request for action. It requires my whole being – all of me. It means that God is my priority. He is foremost in my thoughts. He is my central focus. But loving God is a choice:

- He desires we love Him to the core of our being. (*heart*)
- He desires that we love Him with all our emotions. (*soul*)
- He wants us to love Him with all our energy. (*strength*)
- He desires that we willfully choose to love Him. (*mind*)

Thus, our love should be sincere and genuine. It is true and real in our lives. It should also be strong (intense and passionate). It has to be intentional or apathy and laziness can seep into the relationship. Lastly it has to be active for the same reasons it must be intentional. Being active means you are engaged and involved.

Q1. What does love mean to you? How would you summarize loving God for <u>your</u> own understanding?

We make a choice to love God. All other issues related to God are dependent on the quality of our love relationship with Him. John 14:15 says that if you claim to love God, then you will obey His commands. Thus, our relationship should be characterized by deep sincerity, integrity, loyalty, and true commitment. It should not be based on superficial religious activity (e.g. doing good works because that is what a Christian does).

The Love Chapter (1 Corinthians 13) tells us all we should need to know about the nature of love:

It is patient: is enduring, tolerant, uncomplaining, long-suffering, or calm
It is kind: is caring, thoughtful, helpful, good, considerate, and concerned
It does not envy: is not jealous, holds no resentment
It does not boast: does not brag, show off, or act like a know-it-all
It is not proud: is not arrogant, conceited, pompous, or big-headed
It is not rude: is courteous, polite, respectful; not boorish or vulgar
It is not self-seeking: is humble; not selfish, self-absorbed, or egotistical
It is not easily angered: is self-controlled, composed, peaceable, calm
It does not record wrongs: is forgiving, tolerant, and magnanimous
It does not delight in evil: dislikes evil; does not take pleasure in evil
It loves the truth: is honest, keeps promises, has integrity, is trustworthy
It protects: defends, guards, shields, cares for, watches over
It trusts: has faith in, has hope in, believes in, depends upon
It hopes: has faith; does not despair, is not despondent
It perseveres: persists, keeps at it, sticks with it, carries on, does not quit

Q2. What would you conclude about love from 1 Cor 13?

In 1 Corinthians 13, Paul says that if a person doesn't have love, then he is just sounding brass or a clanging cymbal. Paul makes it very clear that we must have love above all other things. He says in 13:3, *"If I give away all I have, and if I deliver up my body to be burned, but have not love, I gain nothing."* ESV

Paul further indicates that love never fails and that love is greater than being able to prophesy (preach/teach), to have charismatic gifts, or to be given a word of knowledge. Love must simply accompany all we do and say and when it doesn't, God is dishonored.

OBSERVATIONS

The word "love" appears over 500 times in the Bible and as often in the Old Testament as the New Testament. Since this word is so widely used I have chosen Scriptures only from John and 1 John for review. What do you learn from the following?

John 13:34-35 *A new commandment I give to you, that you love one another: just as I have loved you, you also are to love one another. 35 By this all people will know that you are my disciples, if you have love for one another.* ESV

Love proves we are disciples! Are we disciples? Do our friends know or suspect we are Christians? Why? The Bible says that when we meet Jesus there will be those who say, "Lord, Lord, haven't we done wonderful things in your name?" And the Lord will say, "Depart from me. I never knew you" (see Matthew 7:22–23). What will determine if we are known by God? Good works? Faith? The Bible says there is only one way to know for sure a person is a Christian: If you have love for one another.

Q3a. Why do you think "loving one another" is the indicator?

Q3b. Note the following from John's gospel. What are we to do?

John 14:15, 24 *If you love me, you will keep my commandments . . . 24 Whoever does not love me does not keep my words. And the word that you hear is not mine, but the Father who sent me.* ESV

John 15:10, 12, 17 *If you keep my commandments, you will abide in my love, just as I have kept my Father's commandments and abide in his love . . . 12 This is my commandment, that you love one another as I have loved you . . . 17 These things I command you, so that you will love one another.* ESV

Q4. What is the challenge in John 15:12?

Q5. What does it mean that "Anyone who does not love abides in death?"

1 John 3:10-11, 14 *By this it is evident who are the children of God, and who are the children of the devil: whoever does not practice righteousness is not of God, nor is the one who does not love his brother. 11 For this is the message that you have heard from the beginning, that we should love one another . . . 14 We know that we have passed out of death into life, because we love the brothers.* <u>*Whoever does not love abides in death.*</u> ESV

Identify from 1 John below what we are <u>not</u> to do.

1 John 2:15 *Do <u>not</u> love the world or the things in the world. If anyone loves the world, the love of the Father is not in him.* ESV

1 John 3:18 *Little children, let us <u>not</u> love in word or talk but in deed and in truth.* ESV

1 John 4:7-8 *Beloved, let us love one another, for love is from God, and whoever loves has been born of God and knows God. 8 Anyone who does <u>not</u> love does not know God, because God is love . . .* ESV

1 John 4:18-20 *There is <u>no</u> fear in love, but perfect love casts out fear. For fear has to do with punishment, and whoever fears has not been perfected in love. 19 We love because he first loved us. 20 If anyone says, "I love God," and hates his brother, he is a liar ; for he who does <u>not</u> love his brother whom he has seen cannot love God whom he has not seen.* ESV

Q6. How might you summarize the above relative to loving God?

What are the major themes? What did you learn? Are there any hints about what it means to love God? Record any significant conclusions in the "SUMMARY: Loving God" section, later in this chapter.

LOVE IS THE *GREATEST COMMANDMENT*

Paul says in 1 Corinthians 13:13 that when all is said and done there are three foundational attributes: faith, hope and love. But even then Paul indicates that the most import one of these is love.

> *And now these three remain:*
> *faith, hope and love.*
> *And the greatest of these is love.*

Q7. In <u>your</u> opinion why does Paul come to this conclusion? How would you argue that this is true?

Q8. Why wouldn't faith be the greatest commandment?

THE FRUIT OF THE SPIRIT

But the fruit of the Spirit is love, joy, peace, patience, kindness, goodness, faithfulness, gentleness, self-control . . .
(Galatians 5:22-23 ESV)

One might argue that love is not only the first attribute listed as being part of the fruit of the Spirit, but love is an integral part of each of the other characteristics. If we compare the fruit with the attributes of love listed in 1 Corinthians 13 we find a very close correlation to Galatians 5:22-23.

> *4 Love is patient, love is kind. It does not envy, it does not boast, it is not proud.*
> *5 It is not rude, it is not self-seeking, it is not easily angered, it keeps no record of wrongs.*
> *6 Love does not delight in evil but rejoices with the truth.*
> *7 It always protects, always trusts, always hopes, always perseveres.* (1 Corinthians 13:4-7 NIV)

Using 1 Corinthians 13:4-7, fill in the blanks below:

<u>Fruit Characteristic</u>   <u>Where found in 1 Cor 13:4-7</u>

KINDNESS: Love is _____ (13:4).

GOODNESS: Love is kind, it does not _____,
              it does not _____ (13:4).

GENTLENESS: Love is not _____.
              It is not _____. (13:4-5)

PEACE: Love is not easily _____ (13:5).

JOY: Love does not _____ in evil,
              but _____with the truth (13:6).

PATIENCE: Love is_____ (13:4).
              Love always _____ (13:7).

FAITH: Love always _____ and
              always _____ (13:7).

Q9. What conclusions might you draw knowing the degree to which love is an inherent part of the fruit of the Spirit?

FEAR OF THE LORD

Love is linked to another very important concept in the following verses.

> **Psalms 147:11** but the Lord takes pleasure in those who <u>fear</u> him, in those who hope in his steadfast love. ESV

> **Psalms 103:11** For as high as the heavens are above the earth, so great is his steadfast love toward those who <u>fear</u> him . . . ESV

> **Psalms 103:17** But the steadfast love of the Lord is from everlasting to everlasting on those who <u>fear</u> him, and his righteousness to children's children . . . ESV

> **Psalms 118:4** Let those who <u>fear</u> the Lord say, "His steadfast love endures forever." ESV

> **1 Peter 2:17** Honor everyone. Love the brotherhood. <u>Fear</u> God. Honor the emperor. ESV

The concept is: *the fear of the Lord.*

What does this mean and what are the implications relative to the *love* that is mentioned? In answering this question remember Solomon's conclusion about life:

> **Ecclesiastes 12:13-14** The end of the matter; all has been heard. Fear God and keep his commandments, for this is the whole duty of man. 14 For God will bring every deed into judgment, with every secret thing, whether good or evil. ESV

Solomon concluded that it is the <u>whole duty of man</u> to "fear God and keep His commands". If this conclusion is true, one must believe that the concept of "fearing the Lord" is a critical doctrine or principle of God. "Fearing the Lord" is not some obscure phrase that occurs occasionally – it is referenced throughout both the Old and New Testaments by almost all the writers of the Bible.

The fear of the Lord can be described as dreading God's displeasure. We desire His favor, revere His holiness, and submit cheerfully to His will. We are grateful for His benefits, sincerely worship Him, and conscientiously obey His commandments.

Fear in this context is the reverent regard for God, tempered with awe and fear of the punishment for disobedience. It might be described as reverent trepidation or a holy fear and reverence which has its foundation in love and causes one to please God rather than to offend Him. This attitude gives God the place of glory, honor, and reverence He deserves.

SUMMARY: LOVING GOD

Here are five major acts or practices describing what it means to love God. As you study this lesson, add additional practices that demonstrate what it means to love Him.

1 OBEY: If we love then we obey (1 Jn 5:2-3; Jn 14:15, 24)

2 BUILD UP: Enlighten, inform, and encourage others (1 Cor 8)

3 LOVE ONE-ANOTHER: We love our neighbors like He loved us (Jn 15:12, 17; Jn 13:34-35)

4 NOT LOVING THE WORLD: (1 Jn 2:15)

5 DOING GOOD DEEDS: (1 Jn 3:18)

Add any additional practices you identify below:

6 _____
7 _____
8 _____
9 _____
10 _____

Another question that normally arises when considering what it means to love God is "how" do we love Him and "why." Those questions are easily answered from Scripture:

>**HOW:** With all our heart, mind, soul (1 Cor 13)
>
>**WHY**: Because He loved us first (1 Jn 4:19)

Q10. How would you summarize how you think you are doing at loving God?

HINDRANCES

In the real world (in your life) what gets in the way of loving God based on what you have learned in this lesson? What makes success difficult or elusive?

1. What are the hindrances or distractions that you personally battle in trying to love God?

2. Which element is most difficult for you, the decision to love or the actions that result because you love?
Think about this question!

3. In your opinion what are the two most important characteristics you need to practice in order to feel you are adequately loving God?

(1)

(2)

CONCLUSION

Colossians 3:14 (ESV) illustrates how permanent and important love is. Paul uses a picture of a person getting dressed, saying that you can choose anything you want, but "put on love."

> *"And above all these put on love,*
> *which binds everything together*
> *in perfect harmony."*

Joshua 23:11 says to be very careful to love God. But that is followed by a warning that if the people disobey the rules and requirements that He, the Lord their God, has given them, then He will not support Israel and they will perish in the land. So there was good reason to be "careful."

How do we acquire this kind of love in our lives today? How can we love God the way He desires? By finding out how much God really loves us. We love Him because He first loved us. He brought us salvation and eternal life. That knowledge needs to rest within our heart and soul. We must make a conscious decision to love Him. Because of what He did for us, we love Him back with all our heart, mind, and strength. He did for us what we could not have done for ourselves!

> *Love is a decision.*
> *Love is not a feeling.*
> *The Bible commands us to love God*
> *and love our brother.*

Prayer

Lord, allow me, help me, and enable me to love you with all my mind, body, heart, soul, and strength! I want a true hunger for a growing, intimate, love relationship with You.

My Personal Prayer

What I Want to Remember

Enter some notes and information that you want to remember about this week's study. It might be a Scripture verse or two, something new you learned, something you want to do, something you want to change, or just something you want to be sure to remember.

Wisdom to Action
Challenge

Does your love for God need work? How much of your heart do you devote to God? Do your best friends know how serious you are about God?

Lesson 8
Obeying God

The life of a Jesus follower can be identified by a number of characteristics describing the nature of his relationship with God. These are not performance activities, but relationship characteristics. They are the stepping stones to establishing, building, and cementing an intimate love relationship with Jesus.

LESSON MEDITATION

Meditate on Solomon's conclusion during your Quiet Time this week.

Ecclesiastes 12:13-14 *The end of the matter; all has been heard. Fear God and keep his commandments, for <u>this is the whole duty of man</u>. 14 For God will bring every deed into judgment, with every secret thing, whether good or evil.* ESV

MEANING OF OBEDIENCE

NOTE: Obedience is an important and extensive subject. We have coved the most important issues in this lesson, but we have examined this subject in much more depth in another book in this series: *The OBEDIENCE of a Jesus Follower: Ignore at your own risk.*

In the Old Testament obedience was critical because being right with God required following God's commandments. It was the ultimate test of faith and reverence, often characterized by the term "fear of the Lord."

In the New Testament a higher spiritual and moral standard is established. For example Matthew 5:22 says, "But I say to you that everyone who is angry with his brother will be liable to judgment. . . ." (ESV) This is a significant challenge relative to our relationship with Christ. We are <u>called</u> to obedience:

> *Through Him we received grace and apostleship*
> *to call all Gentiles to the obedience that comes*
> *from faith for his name sake.*
> Romans 1:5 NIV

Observe that Romans 1:5 says that our obedience comes from faith. Thus if I am a believer and have a relationship with Jesus, I should have a desire to obey.

Q1. What thoughts, images, or actions come to <u>your</u> mind when you think of the word "obedience?"

Q2. If I said that following Jesus is impossible without obedience and that obedience is an absolute requirement, how would you react? If this is a true statement how would you explain it in light of the Gospel?

How can one claim to be a Jesus follower and not obey the teachings of Christ? In this human earth-suit we will always struggle with disobedience, but a true Jesus follower <u>desires</u> to obey God. When a Jesus follower disobeys or lives in rebellion, the Holy Spirit will constantly remind him that what he is doing is not right. We feel guilty when we sin because our conscience bothers us.

And by this we know that we have come to know him, if we keep his commandments. Whoever says "I know him" but does not keep his commandments is a liar, and the truth is not in him . . . (1 John 2:3-4 ESV)

Obedience to God and His Word demonstrates love as well as allows one to draw closer to Christ in an intimate relationship. I choose to keep the commandments because I love Him. <u>*Obedience does not produce love, but love produces obedience!*</u> If we are struggling in our relationship with God, it is not because we have an obedience problem, but because we have a love problem. When I put my worldly needs and desires ahead of God, I fall into fleshly disobedience.

The emphasis in John 14:15, *"If you love me, you will keep my commandments"* (ESV) is on the "loving" part not the obeying part. As I love God more, I will obey more, which will lead to a closer relationship. God wants obedience out of a heart of love, not vain or rote religious duty.

IMPORTANCE OF OBEDIENCE

In the Old Testament we know that obedience was the key factor in determining a right relationship with God because of the Law. What about the New Covenant? In the following section, fill in the blank with the word you think completes the thought based on the Scripture passage.

1) _____ obedience is not acceptable.
James 2:10 *For whoever keeps the whole law but fails in one point has become accountable for all of it.* ESV

2) We are _____ for obedience.
1 Peter 1:2 *God the Father knew you and chose you long ago, and his Spirit has made you holy. As a result, you have obeyed him and have been cleansed by the blood of Jesus Christ.* NLT
[see also Ro 1:5]

3) Obedience is a result/requirement for truly _____ Christ.
1 John 2:3-4 *And by this we know that we have come to know him, if we keep his commandments. 4 Whoever says "I know him" but does not keep his commandments is a liar, and the truth is not in him . . .* ESV

4) Jesus obeyed the Father, thus Jesus is our _____ for obedience.
John 15:10 *If you keep my commandments, you will abide in my love, just as I have kept my Father's commandments and abide in his love.* ESV [see also Heb 5:8]

5) We are to _____ other disciples to obey.
Matthew 28:19-20 *Go therefore and make disciples of all nations, baptizing them in the name of the Father and of the Son and of the Holy Spirit, 20 teaching them to observe all that I have commanded you. And behold, I am with you always, to the end of the age."* ESV [Note the benefit or result identified in Mt 5:19 for teaching obedience]

Q3. In Mt 28:20 we are to teach disciples to obey. How do we do that? How do you teach someone to obey?

Q4. Which verse or verses above are the most challenging or meaningful for you? Why?

TWO KEY VERSES

> **John 15:10** *If you keep my commandments, you will abide in my <u>love</u>, just as I have kept my Father's commandments and <u>abide in his love</u>.* ESV

2 John 6 *And this is <u>love</u>, that we walk according to his commandments; this is the commandment, just as you have heard from the beginning, so that you should walk in it.* ESV

Q5. What is the conclusion from the two verses above?

THE CRITICAL NATURE OF OBEDIENCE

Scripture indicates in other ways the critical nature of obedience? In the following passages we have underlined references to obedience. In the space provided indicate what else you learn about being obedient.

Acts 13:22 *And when he had removed him, he raised up David to be their king, of whom he testified and said, 'I have found in David the son of Jesse a man after my heart, <u>who will do all my will.</u>'* ESV (see also 1Sam 13:13-14)

Jn 15:14 *You are my friends if you <u>do what I command you</u>.* ESV

Q6. Who else in the Bible were considered friends of God?

(a)

(b)

Deut 6:2 *that you may fear the Lord your God, you and your son and your son's son, by <u>keeping all his statutes and his commandments</u>, which I command you, all the days of your life, and that your days may be long.* ESV

Psalms 103:17-18 *But the steadfast love of the Lord is from everlasting to everlasting on those who fear him, and his righteousness to children's children, 18 to those who <u>keep his covenant</u> and remember to <u>do his commandments</u>.* ESV

Q7. Proverbs 19:23 says that "The fear of the Lord leads to life. . . ." What are the implications of this proverb given the above?

Acts 5:27-29 *And when they had brought them, they set them before the council. And the high priest questioned them, 28 saying, "We strictly charged you not to teach in this name, yet here you have filled Jerusalem with your teaching, and you intend to bring this man's blood upon us." 29 But Peter and the apostles answered, "<u>We must obey God rather than men</u>.* ESV

John 14:21, 23 *Whoever has my commandments and keeps them, he it is who loves me. And he who loves me will be loved by my Father, and I will love him and manifest myself to him." . . . 23 Jesus answered him, "If anyone loves me, he will <u>keep my word</u>, and my Father will love him, and we will come to him and make our home with him."* ESV

THE EXAMPLE OF ABRAHAM

Q8. What do you learn from the following passage about obeying God?

Genesis 22:12 *He said, "Do not lay your hand on the boy or do anything to him, for now I know that you fear God, seeing you have not withheld your son, your only son, from me." . . . 16 and said, "By myself I have sworn, declares the Lord, because you have done this and have not withheld your son, your only son, . . . 18 and in your offspring shall all the nations of the earth be blessed, because you have obeyed my voice."* ESV

Q9. Has your obedience ever been tested by God? Explain.

BENEFITS OF OBEDIENCE

Q10. What <u>benefits</u> of obedience can you identify in the following verses?

1 John 3:22 *. . . and whatever we ask we receive from him, <u>because we keep his commandments</u> and do what pleases him.* ESV

Luke 11:28 *But he said, "Blessed rather are those who <u>hear the word of God and keep it</u>!"* ESV

Acts 5:32 *And we are witnesses to these things, and so is the Holy Spirit, whom God has given to <u>those who obey him</u>."* ESV (See also 1 Jn 3:24)

Matthew 12:50 *For whoever <u>does the will of my Father</u> in heaven is my brother and sister and mother."* ESV

Romans 6:16 *Do you not know that if you present yourselves to anyone as <u>obedient slaves</u>, you are slaves of the one whom you obey, either of sin, which leads to death, or of obedience, which leads to righteousness?* ESV

Q11. Which of the benefits above is the most significant benefit to <u>you</u>? Why?

Q12. Do you think the implied obedience requirement for salvation in Mt 12:50 above is an absolute requirement?

JUDGMENT

Note the following verses:

> **2 Thessalonians 1:8** *. . . in flaming fire, inflicting vengeance on those who do not know God and on <u>those who do not obey the gospel</u> of our Lord Jesus.* ESV

Ephesians 5:6 *Let no one deceive you with empty words, for because of these things the wrath of God comes upon the <u>sons of disobedience</u>.* ESV
(See also 1 Pet 4:17; 2 Cor 10:5-6)

Q13. Do these verses resonant with you? How do you react, or what is your response, to verses like this?

HINDRANCES

1. What are the hindrances that you battle in obeying God?

2. In <u>your</u> experience, how do <u>you</u> overcome the distractions hindrances, or temptations that fight against your obedience?

CONCLUSION

Obedience and love for God were requirements right from the beginning. For example:

Deuteronomy 10:12-13 Circumcise Your Heart
And now, Israel, what does the Lord your God require of you, but to fear the Lord your God, to walk in all his ways, to love him, to serve the Lord your God with all your heart and

with all your soul, 13 and to keep the commandments and statutes of the Lord, which I am commanding you today for your good? ESV

Note that in this passage there are two references to obedience. It first says to "walk in all his ways" and then specifically adds the requirement to "keep the commandments and statues of the Lord."

In the New Testament, an even deeper moral and spiritual lifestyle is required to satisfy Christ. Christ illustrated the level of obedience required when He went to the cross. Peter describes believers in Christ as obedient children:

> *As obedient children, do not be conformed to the passions of your former ignorance.*
> 1 Peter 1:14 ESV

A right relationship with God requires obedience in love through faith, by which we become identified as a disciple of Christ. The Gospel of John clearly indicates that Jesus considers "love" a requirement (see Lesson #7), and love is what identifies one as a Christ follower: "*A new commandment I give to you, that you love one another: just as I have loved you, you also are to love one another. By this all people will know that you are my disciples, if you have love for one another.*" (John 13:34-35 ESV).

Notice how John ties love back to obedience in John 14:15, 14:23, and 1 John 5:3 indicating that those who love keep His commandments. The Bible tells us that there are several reasons for one to obey:

- A very deep and intimate faith relationship (Ro 1:5)
- Fear of God's wrath (Eph 5:6; 1 Pet 4:17; 2 Thes 1:8)
- Suffering (Heb 5:8)

I believe the overwhelming characteristic of one who seeks to obey God is that he or she has a deep, abiding, intimate, love relationship with Christ:

> **John 14:15** If you love me, you will keep my commandments. ESV
>
> **John 15:10** If you obey my commandments, you will abide in my love. . . . ESV

Love for God is the key. If we do not love God how can we consistently obey God or even desire to obey Him? If you are struggling with your Christian walk, work on loving and worshiping Him and allow that process to move you to a position of seeking to live in obedience. Ps 112:1 says:

> *"Praise the Lord. Blessed is the man who fears the Lord, who greatly delights in his commandments."* ESV

I want to love God to such an extent that I love His commands, I find great delight (satisfaction) in obeying His Word. My relationship is such that I desire and delight in walking in His presence. His Word is such a part of my existence that my actions automatically follow His commands.

When I mess up, as I surely do from time-to-time, I seek forgiveness and move on. I don't dwell on this or that misstep. I set my eyes on Jesus and don't look back. He is my source of strength and He guides me toward all righteousness.

Prayer: Lord, give me the power and will to obey all Your commands, so that I can truly know and love You. Come Lord Jesus!

My Personal Prayer

What I Want to Remember

Enter some notes and information that you want to remember about this week's study. It might be a Scripture verse or two, something new you learned, something you want to do, something you want to change, or just something you want to be sure to remember.

Wisdom to Action
Challenge

In what area of your life are you struggling with obedience? How can you align your desires more closely with God's will in this specific area?

Lesson 9
Depend on and Trust God

The life of a Jesus follower can be identified by a number of characteristics describing the nature of his relationship with God. These are not performance activities, but relationship characteristics. They are the stepping stones to establishing, building, and cementing an intimate love relationship with Jesus.

LESSON MEDITATION

Meditate on Ps 115:4-11 during your Quiet Time this week.

Psalms 115:4-11 *Their idols are silver and gold. . . . cannot speak . . cannot hear . . cannot feel . . . 8 Those who make them will be like them, and so will all who <u>trust</u> in them. 9 O house of Israel, <u>trust</u> in the LORD – he is their help and shield. 10 O house of Aaron, <u>trust</u> in the LORD – he is their help and shield. 11 You who fear him, <u>trust</u> in the LORD – he is their help and shield.*

DEFINITIONS

Biblical trust is confidence or dependence on God to do what is right or necessary. You know He will do something, even if it is not what you want. The important belief here is that God will do what is right according to His will. His actions will not necessarily be what is right in our eyes. The reality is that we only have a hint of the world around us and that we see dimly. He knows all and will do what is right for His eternal plans.

We could have used the word "faithful" for this characteristic of a Christ follower, but sometimes we confuse our "faith" with "being faithful." One who has accepted Christ as his or her personal Savior has faith, but that does not necessarily mean that such a person is faithful (loyal, dedicated, devoted, steadfast, etc.). So to avoid a tendency for us to feel that we trust and depend on God because we have faith, we have chosen the word *trust* to represent the characteristic of having a firm confidence that because God is trustworthy, we can depend on Him.

A Jesus follower who is faithful trusts and depends on God in the good times and the bad. When I put my trust in God and the truth of the Scriptures, the challenges in my worldly life do not shake my faith or trust in God. Trusting God on a daily basis is only possible if (1) we know His character, and (2) we know His Word. We will trust Him because we know He always keeps His promises. Based on that trust, we can develop an intimate love relationship with Him.

Faith and trust are not generated on their own! Trust is only possible as we know God, know His Word, and become convinced of His faithfulness. Worry, fear, and distrust all result from focusing on our circumstances instead of claiming and depending on God's promises. As we grow in the knowledge of Him and knowledge of the Word of God, we grow in spiritual understanding and develop trust so that we know we can depend on Him when life gets difficult.

> *Trust in the Lord, and do good;*
> *dwell in the land and befriend faithfulness.*
> *Delight yourself in the Lord,*
> *and he will give you the desires of your heart.*
> *Commit your way to the Lord;*
> *trust in him, and he will act.*
> Psalms 37:3-5 ESV

GENERAL

What do you depend on God for? Think of some circumstances when you depended on God to fix or heal a situation. This requires that you really believe that God is faithful, will keep His promise, even if you never see His response or answer to the need as you perceive it. Remember, 1 Cor 10:13 says:

No temptation has overtaken you that is not common to man. God is faithful, and he will not let you be tempted beyond your ability, but with the <u>temptation</u> he will also provide the way of escape, that you may be able to endure it. ESV

Be sure you recognize that this promise here is about temptation. He will provide a way for you to escape the temptation or to endure it. The text is not saying He will help you escape all the trouble you have gotten yourself into.

An obvious question is what type of promises has God made in the Bible? There are many. See the Exhibit at the end of this lesson for a listing of a number of His promises.

Q1. Have you ever asked God to keep a promise? What happened?

WHAT DOES TRUSTING GOD MEAN?

Determine from the following Scriptures what it means to trust God. Summarize your thoughts on each passage at the end.

Psalms 20:7 *Some trust in chariots and some in horses, but <u>we trust in the name of the Lord</u> our God.* ESV

Proverbs 3:5 *<u>Trust in the Lord</u> with all your heart, and do not lean on your own understanding.* ESV

Psalms 37:5 *Commit your way to the Lord; <u>trust in him</u>, and he will act.* ESV

Q2. What does it mean to commit based on Ps 37:5?

Psalms 56:3-4 *When I am afraid, I put my trust in you. 4 In God, whose word I praise, in God I trust; I shall not be afraid. What can flesh do to me?* ESV

Isaiah 8:17 *I will wait for the Lord, who is hiding his face from the house of Jacob, and I will hope (trust) in him.* ESV

John 14:1 *Let not your hearts be troubled. Believe (trust) in God; believe (trust) also in me.* ESV

Philippians 1:6 *And I am sure of this, that he who began a good work in you will bring it to completion at the day of Jesus Christ.*

Summarize the key thoughts in the above verses.
Ps 20:7

Pr 3:5

Ps 37:5

Ps 56: 3-4

Isa 8:17

John 14:1

Phil 1:6

Q3. Is God ever unfaithful? What if we are unfaithful?

Q4. How does one cultivate the ability to trust?

TRUST DISPLAYED IN SCRIPTURE

Q5. Look up the following passages and note how or why someone trusted God.

Gen 6:5-22

Gen 22: 1-12

1 Sam 17:45-47

Daniel 6:23

Q6. How might you describe trust based on the above?

WHAT HAPPENS WHEN WE TRUST?

What happens when we trust God and are faithful to His commands? What are the benefits? What do the following Scriptures tell us about the benefits of trusting God?

Psalms 9:10 *And those who know your name put their trust in you, for you, O Lord, have not forsaken those who seek you.* ESV

Q7. What are the two requirements for trusting in Ps 9:10?

Psalms 37:5-6 *Commit your way to the Lord; trust in him, and he will act. 6 He will bring forth your righteousness as the light, and your justice as the noonday.* ESV

Isaiah 26:3 *You keep him in perfect peace whose mind is stayed on you, because he trusts in you.* ESV

Q8. What is the requirement in Isa 26:3?

Jeremiah 39:18 *For I will surely save you, and you shall not fall by the sword, but you shall have your life as a prize of war, because you have put your trust in me, declares the Lord.* ESV

Romans 15:13 *I pray that God, the source of hope, will fill you completely with joy and peace because you trust in him. Then you will overflow with confident hope through the power of the Holy Spirit.* NLT

Q9. Have you ever experienced any of the benefits above? If so, explain.

SHADRACH, MESHACK, and ABEDNEGO

Q10. What do you learn from the following passage about trusting God?

Daniel 3:17-18 *If this be so, our God whom we serve is able to deliver us from the burning fiery furnace, and he will deliver us out of your hand, O king. 18 But if not, be it known to you, O king, that we will not serve your gods or worship the golden image that you have set up.* ESV

HINDRANCES

1. In your life what gets in the way of trusting God? What makes trust or dependence so elusive?

2. What would make the hindrances go away for you?

3. List the three things (most important for you) that you need to do in order to trust God.

    (1)

    (2)

    (3)

CONCLUSION

God has given us some great and precious promises, but do we actually expect Him to make good on those promises? Do our lives actually reflect that we believe those promises? What actions in your life can you describe that are inconsistent with what you say about your belief in God's faithfulness? Take a minute and note what you do that demonstrates you don't really trust God:

Probably our most significant problem in trusting God is that we tend to think we can fix things ourselves. We depend on self and not on God. We want God to solve our problems but we ignore His commands and requirements. Our pride rears its ugly head and we ignore His laws. We tend to be like Israel during the time of the Judges when they "trusted in their own eyes."

The Book of Hebrews gives us several examples of faith and trust in chapter 11, and then 12:1-3, says:

> **Hebrews 12:1-3** Jesus, Founder and Perfecter of Our Faith *Therefore, since we are surrounded by so great a cloud of witnesses, let us also lay aside every weight, and sin which clings so closely, and let us run with endurance the race that is set before us, 2 looking to Jesus, the founder and perfecter of our faith, who for the joy that was set before him endured the cross, despising the shame, and is seated at the right hand of the throne of God. 3 Consider him who endured from sinners such hostility against himself, so that you may not grow weary or fainthearted.* ESV

We can get no better advice than, "fix your eyes on Jesus." I remember one of the speakers at a Promise Keepers event saying, "I have my eyes on Jesus. I am not looking back. You can do as you like, but as for me, I am following Jesus." Our book in this series titled: *The FOCUS For a Jesus Follower: Keep your eyes fixed on Jesus*, is devoted to this topic.

I think that is good advice. I am going to trust Christ and I am not going to look back. The Bible tells me not to rely on my own strength but to put my trust in the Lord of lords, and the King of kings. Let it be so!

Prayer
Lord, establish my trust in You. Allow your faithfulness to be real to me so that I am totally committed and surrendered to Your ways.

My Personal Prayer

What I Want to Remember

Enter some notes and information that you want to remember about this week's study. It might be a Scripture verse or two, something new you learned, something you want to do, something you want to change, or just something you want to be sure to remember.

Wisdom to Action
Challenge

Identify a current challenge in your life. How can you practically demonstrate your trust in God's character and promises in this situation?

EXHIBIT
Bible Promises (HCSB)

*. . . that not one word has failed of all the good things
that the Lord your God promised concerning you.
All have come to pass for you; not one of them has failed.*
Joshua 23:14 ESV

LOVE
Isaiah 54:10 "Though the mountains move and the hills shake, My love will not be removed from you and My covenant of peace will not be shaken," says your compassionate Lord.

FORGIVENESS
1 John 1:9 If we confess our sins, He is faithful and righteous to forgive us our sins and to cleanse us from all unrighteousness.

PEACE
Romans 5:1 Therefore, since we have been declared righteous by faith, we have peace with God through our Lord Jesus Christ.

JOY
John 16:22 So you also have sorrow now. But I will see you again. Your hearts will rejoice, and no one will rob you of your joy.

ENCOURAGEMENT
Jeremiah 29:11 "For I know the plans I have for you"—this is the Lord's declaration—"plans for your welfare, not for disaster, to give you a future and a hope."

STRENGTH
1 Peter 5:10 Now the God of all grace, who called you to His eternal glory in Christ Jesus, will personally restore, establish, strengthen, and support you after you have suffered a little.

BLESSING
Romans 8:28 We know that all things work together for the good of those who love God: those who are called according to His purpose.

GUIDANCE
John 16:13 When the Spirit of truth comes, He will guide you into all the truth. For He will not speak on His own, but He will speak whatever He hears. He will also declare to you what is to come.

PROTECTION
2 Thessalonians 3:3 But the Lord is faithful; He will strengthen and guard you from the evil one.

NEEDS
Philippians 4:19 And my God will supply all your needs according to His riches in glory in Christ Jesus.

WISDOM
James 1:5 Now if any of you lacks wisdom, he should ask God, who gives to all generously and without criticizing, and it will be given to him.

DESPAIR
Psalms 46:1 God is our refuge and strength, a helper who is always found in times of trouble.

FEAR
Hebrews 13:6 Therefore, we may boldly say: The Lord is my helper; I will not be afraid. What can man do to me?

DISAPPOINTMENT
Isaiah 49:23 . . . Then you will know that I am the Lord; those who put their hope in Me will not be put to shame (*disappointed*).

DEPRESSION
Romans 15:13 Now may the God of hope fill you with all joy and peace in believing, so that you may overflow with hope by the power of the Holy Spirit.

WORRY
Philippians 4:6-7 Don't worry about anything, but in everything, through prayer and petition with thanksgiving, let your requests be made known to God. 7 And the peace of God, which surpasses every thought, will guard your hearts and your minds in Christ Jesus.

CONFUSION
Psalms 32:8 I will instruct you and show you the way to go; with My eye on you, I will give counsel.

TEMPTATION
1 Corinthians 10:13 No temptation has overtaken you except what is common to humanity. God is faithful and He will not allow you to be tempted beyond what you are able, but with the temptation He will also provide a way of escape, so that you are able to bear it.

GRIEVE
Matthew 5:4 Blessed are those who mourn, because they will be comforted.

Lesson 10
Walk Humbly With Your God
(Live in submission)

The life of a Jesus follower can be identified by a number of characteristics describing the nature of his relationship with God. These are not performance activities, but relationship characteristics. They are the stepping stones to establishing, building, and cementing an intimate love relationship with Jesus.

LESSON MEDITATION

Meditate on the following during your Quiet Time this week.

Matthew 18:3-4 *"Truly, I say to you, unless you turn and become like children, you will never enter the kingdom of heaven. 4 Whoever humbles himself like this child is the greatest in the kingdom of heaven.* ESV

DEFINITIONS

Generally being humble means you have a spirit of deference. You are concerned about the needs of others as much as your own. You are not proud, arrogant, or conceited. In a Biblical sense walking humbly with our God means:

- You are not arrogant or pretentious.
- You act with spirit of deference or submission.
- You respect, honor, and esteem God.
- You openly recognize the need to trust in Him.

CALL TO HUMILTY

Zeph 2:3
Calls us to seek the LORD and humility.

Jeremiah 44:10
Expects us to humble ourselves.

Ephesians 4:2
Instruct us to be humble and gentle.

Colossians 3:12
Tells us to clothe ourselves with kindness and humility.

Titus 3:2
Expects us to show humility toward all men.

Romans 11:20-21
Tells us not to be arrogant, but afraid.

It seems clear that God desires followers that are humble. This desire for humility should not be surprising since Jesus is humble and we are being made into His likeness (2 Cor 3:17-18 and Ro 8:29). Since we are being conformed to the likeness of Christ, we will become like Him in godly character, including humility. From a spiritual perspective, humility is the ability to think of others as more important than yourself or more highly than yourself. The focus is on others, not self. This attitude toward God is what He desires from all His followers.

James describes humility in 1:9-10 saying that those in lowly positions ought to take pride or be thankful in that circumstance and not feel inferior, and those who are rich or in high positions should take pride in circumstances that bring them to a "low position." We should not take pride in wealth, position, or accomplishments, and if we desire to boast we should boast about knowing God. James further suggests in 3:13 that the deeds we do should be done in humility. Doing good deeds should honor Christ and exalt God, not be a source of pride and boasting. We should be willing to do work in the background without receiving recognition.

Paul speaks about being humble in Romans 12:16, where he indicates that we are to live in harmony with one another, associating with all kinds of people regardless of their social station in life. He declares that we should "not be conceited."

> *Take my yoke upon you, and learn from me,*
> *for I am gentle and lowly in heart,*
> *and you will find rest for your souls.*
> Mt 11:29 ESV

Q1. How would you describe what Jesus means in Mt 11:29?

Q2. What do you think a relationship with Christ would be like if He was <u>not</u> humble?

HUMILITY TOWARD GOD

Philippians 2:3 says, *"Do nothing from rivalry or conceit, but in humility count others more significant than yourselves."* ESV How does that work? Humility can seem almost like a divine attribute, a character trait that is so far removed from our reality that achievement seems improbable.

From each of the verses below determine and record what Scripture tells us about walking in humility.

Philippians 2:8 *And being found in human form, he humbled himself by becoming obedient to the point of death, even death on a cross.* ESV

Q3. Other than going to the Cross, can you think of an example of when Jesus displayed humility?

Romans 12:3 *For by the grace given to me I say to everyone among you not to think of himself more highly than he ought to think, but to think with sober judgment, each according to the measure of faith that God has assigned.* ESV

Q4. What does it mean to think of yourself with "sober judgment?"

1 Thessalonians 5:18 tells us we are to give thanks for all circumstances (good and bad). An attitude of thanksgiving for life no matter the situation recognizes that God is in control and He is overseeing your life and if He is going to allow something in your life, then who are you to suggest God is wrong.

HUMILITY TOWARD ONE ANOTHER

Walking humbly includes being humble toward one another. How do the following passages tell us to be humble.

Luke 14:10-11 *But when you are invited, go and sit in the lowest place, so that when your host comes he may say to you, 'Friend, move up higher.' Then you will be honored in the presence of all who sit at table with you. 11 For everyone who exalts himself will be humbled, and he who humbles himself will be exalted.* ESV

Hebrews 13:17 *Obey your leaders and submit to them, for they are keeping watch over your souls, as those who will have to give an account. Let them do this with joy and not with groaning, for that would be of no advantage to you.* ESV

1 Peter 5:5 *Likewise, you who are younger, be subject to the elders. Clothe yourselves, all of you, with humility toward one another, for "God opposes the proud but gives grace to the humble."* ESV

Matthew 5:38-39 *You have heard that it was said, 'An eye for an eye and a tooth for a tooth.' 39 But I say to you, Do not resist the one who is evil. But if anyone slaps you on the right cheek, turn to him the other also.* ESV

Micah 6:8 *He has told you, O man, what is good; and what does the Lord require of you but to do justice, and to love kindness, and to <u>walk humbly with your God</u>?* ESV

Q5. Do you think this passage is an adequate and sufficient requirement for being totally right with God? If not, what is missing?

Ephesians 4:1-2 *I therefore, a prisoner for the Lord, urge you to walk in a manner worthy of the calling to which you have been called, 2 with all humility and gentleness, with patience, bearing with one another in love,* ESV

We should recognize that in the Old Testament the implied requirement is the keeping of the Law. In the New Testament the implication is that it is part of our calling. These passages are both very clear indications that God desires humility to be an important characteristic of our relationship with Him and with one another.

PRIDE

Pride is inordinate and unreasonable self-esteem associated with insolence and the rude treatment of others. The Bible characterizes it as follows:

- Pride tries to ignore God (Ps 10:4) and prefers to trust in what is deceptive and empty (Ps 40:4).

- Pride is associated with wickedness and injustice (Ps 94:2-7; Prov 21:3; Job 40:11).

- Pride is the opposite of wisdom (Prov 8:12), patience (Eccl 7:8), and humility (Prov 11:2; James 4:6; 1 Peter 5:5).

- The proud tell contemptuous lies against the righteous (Ps 31:1 and 59:12ff).

As in the Old Testament, so also in the New Testament, pride is associated with other vices. In Mark 7:22 haughtiness is listed with the sins of envy, slander, and foolishness and in 2 Tim 3:2 bragging is mentioned with love of self, love of money, arrogance, and abusiveness. 1 John 2:16 links pride with lust.

Thus the proud person offends God by his self-exaltation.

Q6. What do you learn or observe about pride or arrogance in the following verses?

Malachi 4:1 *For behold, the day is coming, burning like an oven, when all the <u>arrogant</u> and all evildoers will be stubble. The day that is coming shall set them ablaze, says the Lord of hosts, so*

that it will leave them neither root nor branch. ESV
(See also Isa 2:17 and 13:11)

2 Chronicles 32:25 *But Hezekiah did not make return according to the benefit done to him, for his heart was proud. Therefore wrath came upon him and Judah and Jerusalem.* ESV

Proverbs 16:18 *Pride goes before destruction, and a haughty spirit before a fall.* ESV

Proverbs 6:16-17 *There are six things that the Lord hates, seven that are an abomination to him: haughty eyes, a lying tongue . . .* ESV [see also Proverbs 8:13]

Q7. What seems clear from these four verses if we are prideful?

It should be observed that the pronouncement of judgments about the lack of humility ring out from Scripture very clearly. The Proverbs state that the LORD *hates* pride. In the New Testament James speaks very directly about humility:

*Therefore put away all filthiness and rampant
wickedness and receive with meekness the
implanted word, which is able to save your souls.*
James 1:21 ESV

Pride can prevent us from making life changing decisions or encourage us to make the wrong decisions. We must humbly accept and follow God's Word because it can protect save us.

Q8. Do you think one can accept the call of Christ without being or becoming humble?

BENEFITS OF WALKING HUMBLY

Q9. What benefits can you identify in the following verses for walking humbly with your God?

Isaiah 66:2 *All these things my hand has made, and so all these things came to be, declares the Lord. But this is the one to whom I will look: he who is humble and contrite in spirit and trembles at my word.* ESV

Proverbs 3:34 *Toward the scorners he is scornful, but to the humble he gives favor.* ESV

Psalms 147:6 *The Lord lifts up the humble; he casts the wicked to the ground.* ESV

Psalms 25:9 *He leads the humble in what is right, and teaches the humble his way.* ESV

Luke 18:14 *. . . For everyone who exalts himself will be humbled, but the one who humbles himself will be exalted."* ESV

All the benefits above come from God for being humble. In addition, both James (4:10) and Peter (1 Pet 5:7) say that if we humble ourselves before the Lord, or under God's mighty presence, "He will lift you up." Both these passages are surrounded with exhortations to live according to God's wishes and commands. Those who can live humbly under God's instructions will receive grace, power over sin, freedom from anxiety, and be "lifted up."

But humility does not mean we should have no self-esteem or ignore our own needs. We should not overreact to Solomon's words in Ecclesiastes that all is vanity. But we should be free from vanity and conceit. We are not to be empty or futile but live under the promises of God, internally knowing that we have a high calling, but not exhibiting an attitude of superiority.

It's worthwhile to note what God says to Israel through the prophet Isaiah. God speaks of those people He esteems or those He holds in high regard. He values those who are humble and contrite (Isa 66:2). The prophet Micah relates the same message to Israel: "walk humbly with your God" (Micah 6:8). God is serious about His desire for us to act and walk humbly in our life journey. Jesus says the same thing in a different way in Matthew 18:15. The disciples wanted to know who was the greatest in the kingdom of heaven. Jesus answered them by indicating they would need to become like little children.

SUBMISSION

Another word describing a humble relationship with God is "*submission*." To submit to someone means:

- to yield oneself to the authority or will of another
- to permit oneself to be subjected to another
- to defer to the opinion or authority of another

The Bible indicates that a Christ follower should submit to the authority of Christ. It could not be more clearly stated than in James 4:7 where it says we are to "submit" ourselves to God. But problems can develop when Jesus followers don't have a solid foundation in their faith:

> **Romans 8:7** *For the mind that is set on the flesh is hostile to God, for it does <u>not submit to God's law</u>; indeed, it cannot.* ESV

> **Romans 10:2-3** *I bear them witness that they have a zeal for God, but not according to knowledge. 3 For, being ignorant of the righteousness that comes from God, and seeking to establish their own, they did <u>not submit to God's righteousness</u>.* ESV

Scripture is quite clear that Christ is the head of the church. 1 Cor 11:3 says that that the head of every man is Christ and Eph 5:24 confirms that the church submits itself to Christ. Heb 12:9 compares it with the submission we exhibit with human fathers.

CONCLUSION

One of the scary things about the subject of humility is that Proverbs says that God hates those with haughty eyes (exhibiting pride), and He hates pride and arrogance (Pr 6:16-17; Prov 8:13). The biggest danger of pride comes when we are successful or satisfied with life. There are two passages in the Old Testament that describe this danger:

> **Deuteronomy 8:12-14** *Otherwise, when you eat and are satisfied, when you build fine houses and settle down, 13 and when your herds and flocks grow large and your silver and gold increase and all you have is multiplied, 14 then your heart will become proud and you will forget the LORD your God, who brought you out of Egypt, out of the land of slavery.* NIV

> **Hosea 13:6** *When I fed them, they were satisfied; when they were satisfied, they became proud; then they forgot me.* NIV

When life is treating us well we tend to think we produced or achieved that state ourselves and we forget that God provided it and that He can take it away, if necessary. We also tend to think that we are the ones that produced the good things in life and we really don't need help navigating the rough rivers of life. Humility does not mean we have low self-esteem, but that we exhibit traits like "gentleness" and "meekness" which express the obedient and humble nature of our relationship with Christ.

In summary humility means we would:

- not allow pride to drive our actions
- not put our needs ahead of the desires of God
- serve others, rather than be served
- not take credit
- pray that God be glorified through us

The key to living in humility before God is understanding and acting on the fact that we can do nothing of eternal value on our own – we must depend on God. Thus, we walk in humble obedience. If we think we did it and don't need help living the Christian life, then we are likely headed for a fall.

DISCUSSION AND THOUGHT QUESTIONS

1. In the real world your life gets in the way of being humble before God? What makes submission difficult for you personally?

2. For you personally, what would help or increase your ability to walk humbly with God?

3. In <u>your</u> opinion what are the three most important characteristics of a person who successfully lives in submission to Christ? Why?

      a.

      b.

      c.

4. When is the last time you demonstrated humility that another person would have observed?

5. Do you think one can learn to be humble?

6. Have you ever got yourself into trouble by being proud?

7. When is the last time you boasted? What was it about? Have you ever boasted about knowing God?

Prayer

Lord, I need you, every hour I need you. I need you to provide wisdom so that I make godly choices. I need you to keep me on the narrow road. I need you to teach and guide me in righteousness. I need you to walk in humble obedience. Come Lord Jesus.

My Personal Prayer:

What I Want to Remember

Enter some notes and information that you want to remember about this week's study. It might be a Scripture verse or two, something new you learned, something you want to do, something you want to change, or just something you want to be sure to remember.

Wisdom to Action
Challenge

In what area of your life do you need to cultivate more humility? What specific action can you take to walk more humbly with God this week?

Lesson 11
Enjoy God

The life of a Jesus follower can be identified by a number of characteristics describing the nature of his relationship with God. These are not performance activities, but relationship characteristics. They are the stepping stones to establishing, building, and cementing an intimate love relationship with Jesus.

LESSON MEDITATION

Meditate on the following during your Quiet Time this week.

John 15:7-11 *If you abide in me, and my words abide in you, ask whatever you wish, and it will be done for you. 8 By this my Father is glorified, that you bear much fruit and so prove to be my disciples. 9 As the Father has loved me, so have I loved you. Abide in my love. 10 If you keep my commandments, you will abide in my love, just as I have kept my Father's commandments and abide in his love. 11 These things I have spoken to you, that my joy may be in you, and that your joy may be full.* ESV

DEFINITIONS

In general when you enjoy something or receive joy it means you are taking pleasure in something. It gives you satisfaction or contentment. It may be a good time, good music, good food, etc. In the Biblical sense you might associate joy with the word "delight." Psalm 37:4 may come to mind where it says to take delight in God and He will give you the desires of your heart. That statement alone should produce great joy for you.

FREEDOM

For the purpose of this study we will consider that enjoying God and having joy in the Christian life are the same. Thus, in examining the characteristics of a Jesus follower we will look at what brings joy, peace, contentment, etc. The Jesus follower has a foundation of *freedom* that allows him to rest in the joy of the Lord. Because the question of salvation has been settled, the challenge for the Jesus follower is, "How do I thrive in this evil world?" Paul confirms our "freedom" in many passages and the following is typical:

> *It is for freedom that Christ has set us free. Stand firm, then, and do not let yourselves be burdened again by a yoke of slavery . . . You, my brothers, were called to be free. But do not use your freedom to indulge the sinful nature; rather, serve one another in love.* (Gal 5:1, 13 NIV) See also Eph 3:12-13 and 1 Peter 2:16-17.

REJOICE & DELIGHT IN THE LORD

The following passages confirm that there is to be joy in our relationship with Christ. What else do you learn?

1 Chronicles 16:10 *Glory in his holy name; let the hearts of those who seek the Lord rejoice!* ESV

Psalms 16:11 *You make known to me the path of life; in your presence there is fullness of joy; at your right hand are pleasures forevermore.* ESV

Psalms 32:11 *Be glad in the Lord, and rejoice, O righteous, and shout for joy, all you upright in heart!* ESV

Psalms 37:4 *Delight yourself in the Lord, and he will give you the desires of your heart.* ESV

Philippians 4:4 *Rejoice in the Lord always; again I will say, Rejoice.* ESV

True abiding joy is only found in an intimate love relationship with Jesus. When we have a close relationship with Christ, God's will or plan for our lives will match our wants and desires. Following Jesus is not a journey of drudgery, but the pathway to experiencing real joy. This type of joy is revealed in a Jesus follower through authentic praise, thanksgiving, and peace. Our enjoyment of God is determined by the depth of our relationship with Jesus, not by our circumstances in life.[5]

WORRY AND CONCERN

Worry and concern should not rock your boat! Why should you worry if you can experience the joy of the Lord?

> **Matthew 6:25, 33-34** *Therefore I tell you, do not be anxious about your life, what you will eat or what you will drink, nor about your body, what you will put on. Is not life more than food, and the body more than clothing? . . . 33 But seek first the kingdom of God and his righteousness, and all these things will be added to you. 34 Therefore do not be anxious about tomorrow, for tomorrow will be anxious for itself. Sufficient for the day is its own trouble.* ESV

> **Philippians 4:6** *. . . do not be anxious about anything, but in everything by prayer and supplication with thanksgiving let your requests be made known to God.* ESV

Q1. If you are a Jesus follower, what do you have to worry about?

If you look closely at the two passages above it would be relatively hard to find something you should worry about!

Q2. What is the nature of what <u>you</u> worry about? Do you worry about your health, finances, job, family, or do you worry about: (1) losing your salvation, (2) being punished by God, (3) not receiving eternal life, or (4) not being able to stand firm in your faith?

PEACE

The Bible has a lot to say about peace. When Jesus was born the heavenly host praised God and said, "And peace on earth to people He favors." Jesus brought peace, meaning tranquility, unity, and harmony with God to the earth. His peace did not necessarily refer to the kind of peace where no evil exists, but the kind where we trust in and have faith in God resulting in peace. Our hope and confidence in Christ overshadows all worries about the difficulties of life. It quiets our nervous soul and we rest in the knowledge of a faithful and loving God.

In Romans 5:1 Paul says we have peace with God because we have been justified by faith. Because we know that we have been made right with God by our faith, we can live in the freedom of that knowledge. The following passages confirm the peace of God. Record below what else we are told to do?

John 14:27 *Peace I leave with you; my peace I give to you. Not as the world gives do I give to you. Let not your hearts be troubled, neither let them be afraid.* ESV

Philippians 4:6-7 . . . *do not be anxious about anything, but in everything by prayer and supplication with thanksgiving let your requests be made known to God. 7 And the peace of God, which surpasses all understanding, will guard your hearts and your minds in Christ Jesus.* ESV

Q3. What does "the peace of God" in Php 4:7 mean to you?

JOY

The world today generally does not distinguish between happiness and joy. People of the world demand instant gratification and feelings of happiness at their calling.

In contrast, Christian joy does not come from performance or circumstances but rather because of the knowledge, grace, and goodness of God. This earth is not my home. I am just passing through, and everything of value ultimately rests in the assurance of my salvation. It is the peace of God that produces a calm assurance or serenity in my present circumstances which comes about because of my relationship with Christ.

So, where does joy come from? It comes from the grace and the goodness of God. We may experience trials, hardship, or suffering but they should not impact our joy. We may not be happy. We may be very sad, we may even be grieving. But nothing should impact our joy.

The Biblical view of joy is the composed state of the mind that results because I understand my God, my faith, and my relationship with God. Peter describes this as an inheritance:

> **1 Peter 1:1, 4, 8-9** . . . *to an inheritance that is imperishable, undefiled, and unfading, kept in heaven for you, . . . 8 Though you have not seen him, you love him. Though you do not now see him, you believe in him and rejoice with joy that is <u>inexpressible and filled with glory</u>, 9 obtaining the outcome of your faith, the salvation of your souls.* ESV

With this kind of spiritual inheritance we have a solid foundation for life. Therefore, we can call upon an inner joy that exists in the midst of hardship, trials, discipline, and suffering:

> **2 Corinthians 6:9-10** . . . *we live; as punished, and yet not killed; 10 as sorrowful, yet always rejoicing; as poor, yet making many rich; as having nothing, yet possessing everything.* ESV

The person who does not have a relationship with Christ will not be able to understand the contentment that resides in the heart and soul of a Christ follower. I can be unhappy, sad, and depressed, but that is simply about current circumstances. As the song says, "I have the joy of the Lord deep down in my heart!"

Q4. Have you been at peace in the midst of unrest, trouble, or suffering? Explain.

Q5. How would you describe what the joy in your life results in?

Remember that happiness and joy are not the same. Happiness is based on present circumstances and is temporary in nature. The joy of the Lord is everlasting and not dependent on how you are feeling or the difficulties you might be going through.

CONFIDENCE

Q6. If you ever feel confident, what is that based on?

A Jesus follower has knowledge of His God and the promises of the Bible which give him confidence for the present and the future. In Eph 3:12 Paul says that a Jesus follower can approach God in "freedom and confidence." This confidence comes from God and the faith we have in the Father, Son, and Holy Spirit.

Q7. What do we learn from Hebrews relative to that confidence in the following passages?

Hebrews 4:15-16 *For we do not have a high priest who is unable to sympathize with our weaknesses, but one who in every respect has been tempted as we are, yet without sin. 16 Let us then with <u>confidence</u> draw near to the throne of grace, that we may receive mercy and find grace to help in time of need.* ESV

Hebrews 10:35-36 *Therefore do not throw away your <u>confidence</u>, which has a great reward. 36 For you have need of endurance, so that when you have done the will of God you may receive what is promised.* ESV

Hebrews 13:6 *So we can <u>confidently</u> say, "The Lord is my helper; I will not fear; what can man do to me?"* ESV

Q8. What does the writer of Hebrews mean in 13:6 when he says "what can man do to me?"

Q9. What part of your faith gives you the most confidence?

CONTENTMENT

Q10. What does 1 Tim 6:6-8 mean?

1 Timothy 6:6-8 *Now there is great gain in godliness with <u>contentment</u>, 7 for we brought nothing into the world, and we cannot take anything out of the world. 8 But if we have food and clothing, with these we will be <u>content</u>.* ESV

Q11. What do we learn from Php 4:11-13 about contentment?

Philippians 4:11-13 *Not that I am speaking of being in need, for I have learned in whatever situation I am to be content. 12 I know how to be brought low, and I know how to abound. In any and every circumstance, I have learned the secret of facing plenty and hunger, abundance and need. 13 I can do all things through him who strengthens me.* ESV

Q12. How would you describe what the above passage means to you?

HOPE

In secular society, to "hope" in or for something means we want it to happen or to be true. There is usually some expectation that it *might* come true. "Hope" in the Biblical sense means that we have a *confident expectancy* in something. In the Bible the word does not arise because man wants something, but rather is associated with God and what He will do. In many situations the word faith could be substituted for hope in the Biblical text. For example:

> **1 Peter 1:3** Born Again to a Living Hope
> *Blessed be the God and Father of our Lord Jesus Christ! According to his great mercy, he has caused us to be born again to a <u>living hope</u> through the resurrection of Jesus Christ from the dead . . .* ESV

Therefore the "hope" is either in God or in what He will do in the future for the Jesus follower.

Q13. What is the object of our hope in the following passages?

Titus 3:7 *. . . so that being justified by his grace we might become heirs according to the <u>hope</u> of eternal life.* ESV

1 Thessalonians 5:8 *But since we belong to the day, let us be sober, having put on the breastplate of faith and love, and for a helmet the <u>hope</u> of salvation.* ESV

Galatians 5:5 *For through the Spirit, by faith, we ourselves eagerly wait for the <u>hope</u> of righteousness.* ESV

Acts 23:6 *Now when Paul . . . cried out in the council, "Brothers, I am a Pharisee, a son of Pharisees. It is with respect to the <u>hope</u> and the resurrection of the dead that I am on trial."* ESV

In addition 2 Thessalonians 2:16 says that God gives us eternal encouragement along with our hope. The objects of our hope based on the above passages are eternal life, salvation, righteousness, and the resurrection from the dead. This should produce joy resulting in worship and praise for the Lord our God!

Those who have hope in Jesus have great expectations for their spiritual future, and that produces a foundation of joy. That joy allows one to live and function in a world that is in chaos or even thrive in the midst of evil. That inner joy can be infectious to those around you resulting in the power to live triumphantly while others struggle. The hope of the righteous is in the power of God.

Romans 15:13 says that we can abound (overflow) in hope. That hope fills us with joy and that joy will overflow to the benefit of others and praise to God.

PERSONAL REFLECTION

1. Based on this lesson, do you enjoy God? Why? Why not?

2. How has the enjoyment or lack of enjoyment of God impacted your life?

3. In the real world (in your life) what gets in the way of enjoying God? What makes enjoyment, peace, or being content difficult or elusive?

CONCLUSION

Enjoying God means I am not worried or concerned about my "Christian performance." I understand that God loves me regardless of how well or how poorly I am serving Him. I do not have to sit around wondering if I should be doing this or that for Christ in order to maintain my Christian standing.

I just have to be working on my relationship with Him. If I am to feel guilty about anything it should be that I am not spending enough time with Him. If you look back over the relationship characteristics we have been studying the last eleven weeks it is all about relationship, not about working or serving. Serving will flow naturally out of the love relationship we have for Christ.

The one subject we have not yet covered that occurs when one has a right relationship with God is praise and worship. We have saved that for last in the series of subjects of relationship characteristics because true and genuine worship results when we have a right relationship with Christ. That means that the activities we have discussed the past eleven weeks are ongoing in our lives, producing an expression of gratitude and thanksgiving to God that results in praise and worship.

Prayer

Lord, thank you for the freedom I have in Christ. Thank you for paying the sin debt I could not pay for myself. I rejoice in Your presence in my life and hope that what I do will bring You honor and praise. I acknowledge that I have absolutely no reason to worry because You have given me joy, peace, and contentment. Thank you for the hope that gives me confidence to live the life of a Jesus follower in a secular world that is lost. Lord, bring rest to the weary and joy to your people.

My Personal Prayer

What I Want to Remember

Enter some notes and information that you want to remember about this week's study. It might be a Scripture verse or two, something new you learned, something you want to do, something you want to change, or just something you want to be sure to remember.

Wisdom to Action
Challenge

How can you intentionally cultivate a sense of enjoyment in your relationship with God today, even in the midst of challenges?

Lesson 12
Worship God

The life of a Jesus follower can be identified by a number of characteristics describing the nature of his relationship with God. These are not performance activities, but relationship characteristics. They are the stepping stones to establishing, building, and cementing an intimate love relationship with Jesus.

LESSON MEDITATION

Meditate on 1 Chronicles 16:23-30 (David's Psalm of Thanks) during your Quiet Time this week.

23 Sing to the Lord, all the earth; proclaim his salvation day after day.
24 Declare his glory among the nations, his marvelous deeds among all peoples.
25 For great is the Lord and most worthy of praise; he is to be feared above all gods.
26 For all the gods of the nations are idols, but the Lord made the heavens.
27 Splendor and majesty are before him; strength and joy in his dwelling place.
28 Ascribe to the Lord, O families of nations, ascribe to the Lord glory and strength,
29 Ascribe to the Lord the glory due his name. Bring an offering and come before him; worship the Lord in the splendor of his holiness.
30 Tremble before him, all the earth! The world is firmly established; it cannot be moved. NIV

As you meditate on this passage, note all the reasons why we should praise the Lord:

16:23

16:24

16:25

16:26

16:27

16:28

16:29

16:30

Think about what gets in the way of authentic worship for you.

DEFINITION

Worship is the ceremony or response we invoke to express our devotion, allegiance, and honor to God. It can be the direct acknowledgement of His presence, nature, ways, or claims. Worship can be inward (love, joy, trust, adoration, etc.) or it can be expressed outwardly (service, prayer, posture, praise, singing, dancing, giving, etc.).

We cover this subject in more depth in: *The WORSHIP of a Jesus Follower: Is your worship acceptable or in vain?*

AUTHENTIC WORSHIP

How does authentic worship occur? What happens in true worship? The pleasure or joy that comes from magnifying or exalting God occurs because we have an accurate understanding of God. If worship is dry and unsatisfying, it may be because there is a lack of focus on Jesus and the Word of God.

The only worship which honors God is that which is solidly rooted in Biblical truth. Religious feelings or responses that do not come from a true understanding of God are not holy, no matter how intense. Therefore, a person can wave his hands all he wants, but if he doesn't know God or understand what he is doing, and why he is doing it, such responses are likely unacceptable to God because they are unauthentic.

What are the types of responses in worship that are authentic? Perhaps one of the first responses is *stunned silence* because one recognizes or acknowledges the majestic holiness of God (Ps 46:10). One might also sense *awe, wonder, and reverence* at the sheer magnitude of God (Ps 33:8). We are sinful people, therefore, a *holy fear* of God's righteous power might overcome us at some point in true authentic worship (Is 8:13; Ps 5:7). The fear of the Lord can result in *brokenness and contrition* for our ungodly acts (Ps 51:7). Out of these feelings there may arise a deep *longing for God*.

Q1. Are the above responses what you would think might occur in worship? If not, what do you think are more probable responses?

Q2. How do you react to the following Psalm?
Psalms 42:1-2 *As a deer pants for flowing streams, so pants my soul for you, O God. 2 My soul thirsts for God, for the living God. When shall I come and appear before God?* ESV [also Ps 63:1]

A true worshipper longs to experience God Himself, to see Him (like Moses), to know Him, and to be in His presence. When these desires occur, we experience pleasure, joy, and delight. David expressed this in the Psalms:

> **Psalm 16:11** *You make known to me the path of life; in your presence there is fullness of joy; at your right hand are pleasures forevermore.* ESV

Without engaging the heart, we do not truly worship. This engagement produces feelings, emotions, and affections. John Piper says, "Where feelings for God are dead, worship is dead." True worship must include feelings that reflect our gratitude and joy for the love, grace, patience, and mercy of God.

Hypocritical worship is going through the motions (singing, praying, reciting, giving, dancing, etc.) which outwardly indicate affections that do not exist inwardly:

> **Matthew 15:7-9** *You hypocrites! Well did Isaiah prophesy of you, when he said: 8 "This people honors me with their lips, but their heart is far from me; 9 <u>in vain do they worship me</u>, teaching as doctrines the commandments of men."* ESV

If God's truth is revealed to us from His Word or from His creation, and we do not feel in our inner being a longing, hope, fear, dread, joy, or awe, then we may sing, pray, recite, gesture, and give all we want, but it will not be real and authentic worship. Worship reflects back to God the joy that resides within us.

ACCEPTABLE WORSHIP

Did you know that your worship may be rejected by God? What does that mean? If you are like me, I had no idea that my worship could be rejected. It was some years back when this concept hit me. Assuming it was true I began thinking about my attitudes, participation, and thoughts during times of worship and praise. My initial reaction was, "Certainly God won't hold me accountable for my worship!"

The fact is that *our worship can be unacceptable to God*. The first passage below confirms that fact. The last four passages tell us how or why. Record what you learn about acceptable worship:

Hebrews 12:28-29 *Therefore let us be grateful for receiving a kingdom that cannot be shaken, and thus let us offer to God acceptable worship, with reverence and awe, 29 for our God is a consuming fire.* ESV

Malachi 1:8 *When you offer blind animals in sacrifice [worship], is that not evil? And when you offer those that are lame or sick, is that not evil? Present that to your governor; will he accept you or show you favor? says the Lord of hosts.* ESV

Matthew 15:9 *. . . in vain do they worship me, teaching as doctrines the commandments of men.* ESV

John 4:22 *You worship what you do not know; we worship what we know, for salvation is from the Jews.* ESV

Romans 1:22-23 *Claiming to be wise, they became fools, 23 and exchanged the glory of the immortal God for images resembling mortal man and birds and animals and reptiles.* ESV

Worship is the response we invoke to express our devotion, allegiance, and honor to God. Think about your regular worship experience. What are you expressing? How is what you are doing honoring God? These are serious questions that warrant serious thought and may require more time than can be provided in this lesson.

OBSERVATIONS

Q3. What do you learn or observe about the requirements of worship in the following?

Leviticus 9:7 *Then Moses said to Aaron, "Draw near to the altar and offer your sin offering and your burnt offering and make atonement for yourself and for the people, and bring the offering of the people and make atonement for them, as the Lord has commanded."* ESV

Psalms 24:3-4 *Who shall ascend the hill of the Lord? And who shall stand in his holy place? 4 He who has clean hands and a pure heart, who does not lift up his soul to what is false and does not swear deceitfully.* ESV

John 10:9 *I am the door. If anyone enters by me, he will be saved and will go in and out and find pasture.* ESV

Romans 12:1 *I appeal to you therefore, brothers, by the mercies of God, to present your bodies as a living sacrifice, holy and acceptable to God, which is your spiritual worship.* ESV

John 6:35 *Jesus said, "I am the bread of life; whoever comes to me shall not hunger, and whoever believes in me shall never thirst."* ESV

Mark 12:30 *And you shall love the Lord your God with all your heart and with all your soul and with all your mind and with all your strength.* ESV

Q4. Make a list of the four most important instructions in the above passages:

    1.

    2.

    3.

    4.

ATTITUDE OF GRATITUDE

For authentic worship to occur there must be an inherent attitude of gratitude. We come before a mighty, gracious, and loving God and we pour out praise and thanksgiving because of who He is and what He did for us. That praise grows out of an intimate love relationship with Christ. When we find ourselves having difficulty in praise and worship, we should check our gratitude quotient. True authentic worship may be difficult if we are not feeling deeply thankful for what Christ did for us.

Q5. What do the following Scriptures say about how or why we give thanks to God?

Psalms 75:1 *We give thanks to you, O God; we give thanks, for your name is near. . .* ESV

Psalms 106:1 *Praise the Lord! Oh give thanks to the Lord, for he is good, for his steadfast love endures forever!* ESV

2 Corinthians 9:14-15 *. . . while they long for you and pray for you, because of the surpassing grace of God upon you. 15 Thanks be to God for his inexpressible gift!* ESV

Romans 7:24-25 *Wretched man that I am! Who will deliver me from this body of death? 25 Thanks be to God through Jesus Christ our Lord! So then, I myself serve the law of God with my mind, but with my flesh I serve the law of sin.* ESV

1 Corinthians 15:56-57 *The sting of death is sin, and the power of sin is the law. 57 But thanks be to God, who gives us the victory through our Lord Jesus Christ.* ESV

Q6. Based on the above, what are the two gifts of God you are most thankful for? Why?

1.

2.

EXAMINING THE PSALMS

Why look at the psalms? David, who wrote many of the psalms, clearly had a heart for worship and praise. Therefore, it is instructive to examine some of David's psalms:

PSALM 95:1-7 *Come, let us sing for joy to the Lord; let us shout aloud to the Rock of our salvation. 2 Let us come before him with thanksgiving and extol him with music and song. 3 For the Lord is the*

great God, the great King above all gods. 4 In his hand are the depths of the earth, and the mountain peaks belong to him. 5 The sea is his, for he made it, and his hands formed the dry land. 6 Come, let us bow down in worship, let us kneel before the Lord our Maker; 7 for he is our God and we are the people of his pasture, the flock under his care. NIV

    95:1-3 How are we told to worship? _____
    95:4   Why are we to worship? _____
    95:6   How do we show our reverence? _____

PSALMS 96:1-9 *Sing to the Lord a new song; sing to the Lord, all the earth. 2 Sing to the Lord, praise his name; proclaim his salvation day after day. 3 Declare his glory among the nations, his marvelous deeds among all peoples. 4 For great is the Lord and most worthy of praise; he is to be feared above all gods. 5 For all the gods of the nations are idols, but the Lord made the heavens. 6 Splendor and majesty are before him; strength and glory are in his sanctuary. 7 Ascribe to the Lord, O families of nations, ascribe to the Lord glory and strength. 8 Ascribe to the Lord the glory due his name; bring an offering and come into his courts. 9 Worship the Lord in the splendor of his holiness; tremble before him, all the earth.* NIV

    96:1-3 How are we to worship? _____
    96:4-6 Why do we worship? _____
    96:7-8 What are we to ascribe to the Lord? _____
    96:9   What attribute do we recognize and what do we do? ___
    _____

Psalms 98:1-5 *Sing to the Lord a new song, for he has done marvelous things; his right hand and his holy arm have worked salvation for him. 2 The Lord has made his salvation known and revealed his righteousness to the nations. 3 He has remembered his love and his faithfulness to the house of Israel; all the ends of the earth have seen the salvation of our God. 4 Shout for joy to the Lord, all the earth, burst into jubilant song with music; 5 make music to the Lord with the harp, with the harp and the sound of singing . . .* NIV

    98:1   How are we to worship? _____
    98:1-3 Why are we to worship? _____
    98:4-5 How are we to worship? _____

Psalms 99:1-5 *The Lord reigns, let the nations tremble; he sits enthroned between the cherubim, let the earth shake. 2 Great is the Lord in Zion; he is exalted over all the nations. 3 Let them praise your*

great and awesome name — he is holy. 4 The King is mighty, he loves justice — you have established equity; in Jacob you have done what is just and right. 5 Exalt the Lord our God and worship at his footstool; he is holy. NIV

    99:2:   Why do we worship? _____
    99:4   Why do we worship? _____
    99:3, 5 Why do we worship? _____

Psalms 100 Shout for joy to the Lord, all the earth. 2 Worship the Lord with gladness; come before him with joyful songs. 3 Know that the Lord is God. It is he who made us, and we are his; we are his people, the sheep of his pasture. 4 Enter his gates with thanksgiving and his courts with praise; give thanks to him and praise his name.
5 For the Lord is good and his love endures forever; his faithfulness continues through all generations. NIV

    100:1 How are we to worship? _____
    100:2 How are we to worship? _____
    100:3 What do we learn about God? _____
    100:4 How are we to worship? _____
    100:5 Why are we to worship? _____

Q7. Based on these five Psalms, how might you summarize your thoughts on worship?

CONCLUSION

The following seems like a fitting way to end this lesson and our study on being right with God. This is summarized from a book authored by John Piper, *"Let the Nations be Glad!"*

Worship is the ultimate goal of the church. Missions or evangelism is necessary because worship of God is lacking. When this age is over and millions fall on their face before God, missions will no longer be necessary. But worship will continue forever. Our aim in missions is to bring the nations into the white-hot enjoyment of God's glory! The goal is the gladness of the peoples in the greatness of God:

- *The LORD reigns, let the earth be glad; let the distant shores rejoice.* (Ps 97:1 NIV)
- *May the peoples praise you, O God; may all the peoples praise you. May the nations be glad and sing for joy. . .* (Ps 67:3-4 NIV)

Passion for God in worship must precede the offer of God in preaching. You can't recommend what you don't cherish. One cannot say, *"Let the nations be glad,"* if you cannot say from the heart, *"I rejoice in the Lord . . . I will be glad and exult in thee, I will sing praise to thy name, O Most High"* (Ps 104:34; 9:2 NIV).

If the pursuit of God's glory is not ordered above the pursuit of man's good, man will not be well served and God will not be duly honored. Our first priority is to magnify God. When the flame of worship burns with the heat of God's true worth, the light of missions will reach to all parts of the earth. But, where passion for God is weak, zeal for God's work will be weak.

Churches that are not centered on the exultation of the majesty and beauty of God will hardly kindle a fervent desire to *"declare his glory among the nations"* (Ps 96:3). Outsiders will see the disparity between the boldness of our claims and the blandness of our engagement with God.

God must be the central focus of the church. Where people are not stunned by the greatness of God, how can they be sent with the ringing message, *"Great is the Lord and greatly to be praised; he is to be feared above all gods!"* (Ps 96:4)? Savoring the vision of a triumphant loving God in worship precedes spreading it to others. All of history is moving toward one great goal, the worship of God among the peoples of the earth.

> **"The great sin of the world is that we have failed
> to delight in God so to reflect His glory.
> For God is most reflected in us when
> we are most delighted in Him."** John Piper

DISCUSSION QUESTIONS

1. What is "worship" to you? (Review the "technical" definition)

2. Does worship come naturally to you?

3. What does worship produce in you?

Prayer
Lord, I pray for a new and revived passion for worship in my life, for Your presence to manifest itself in my worship. Lord Jesus, I want a seeking heart and a deep desire to know You in worship. Make Yourself known to me in worship, and give me an acute sensitivity to the Spirit during times of worship.

Father, cleanse my heart, mind, and spirit, so that sin cannot interfere with my worship – I want to openly express my love, adoration, and praise for Your greatness. I want an all-consuming hunger to know You in worship. Please eliminate distractions so that I can concentrate only on You. Father, give me a new fervency for Christ.

I ask that your majesty be revealed to me. I want to be stunned by Your greatness. *Great is the Lord and greatly to be praised; He is to be feared above all gods*! May I be overwhelmed by the majesty of Your awesome faithfulness and grace. Halleluiah!

My Personal Prayer

What I Want to Remember

Enter some notes and information that you want to remember about this week's study. It might be a Scripture verse or two, something new you learned, something you want to do, something you want to change, or just something you want to be sure to remember.

Wisdom to Action
Challenge

Beyond Sunday services, how can you incorporate genuine worship into your daily life this week? Consider both your actions and attitude.

Appendix A
Quiet Time

Time: You must find the right time. Your quiet time should last at least half an hour, if possible

Place: Find a place that is quiet and where you can focus and not be bothered.

Materials: Bible; prayer journal or prayer list; paper and pencil

The Process:

Focus: Psalm 46:10, "Be still, and know that I am God." Turn your mind toward God. Think about who he is, what he has done.

Worship: Praise, thanksgiving and/or adoration in prayer, song, or conversation.

The Word: Read or study a passage. [See "Appendix B]

Meditate: Think about what you have read; what does it mean in your life. Is there a command to obey? Is there a promise to claim? Is there a sin to avoid? Is there a lesson to learn?

Record: What is important? What is God saying to you?

Pray: (1) Confession and forgiveness, (2) Pray for others, (3) Pray for self, (4) Worship

Obey: Apply what you have learned or heard to your life.

Appendix B
How To Study The Bible

Before you begin ask the Holy Spirit to reveal God's truth to you.
Ask Him to teach you His ways.

A. Observation — What does the passage say?

1. Read it through several times.
2. Context — Ask "Who, What, When, Where, Why" questions
    a. Who is writing or speaking to whom?
    b. What is happening or being discussed?
    c. Where does the event take place?
    d. When does it take place? Does it relate to other events?
    e. Why is the event taking place? What problems exist?
    f. What comes before and after the passage?
3. Structure: How is the passage organized? Are there significant connecting words?
4. Words: Are words repeated? Is there a key word?
5. Questions to ask:
    a. Does God give any commands or promises in the passage?
    b. What is there to learn about God, Jesus, the Holy Spirit, or other believers?
    c. What comparisons or contrasts are made, if any?
    d. What lists are given?

B. Interpretation — What does it mean?

1. What is being said and what does it mean? What is important?
2. What is the theme? What principles are being taught?

C. Application — What does this mean for my life?

1. How does the it apply to me, my church, my family, or my work?
2. Where do I, my church, or my family fall short?
3. What will I do about it? How do I correct it? Could others help me?
4. What can I do to make this principle an ongoing part of my life?
    a. What attitudes need to be changed?
    b. What actions should I take or avoid?
    c. What promises of God can I claim?
    d. What sins must I confess and forsake?
    e. What examples are there to follow?

Appendix C
What I Want To Remember

For each of 12 weeks we provided space for you to make some notes at the end of the lesson for what you might want to remember from the study. You may or may not have done that. Following are my personal notes when I did this study for the first time.

Week 1 – We are **LOVED** by God.

1. God's love for me will not change, regardless of how good or bad my performance.
2. Zeph 3:17 . . . He will rejoice over you with singing.

Week 2 – We are called to a **RELATIONSHIP**.

1. Mt 7:21-23 ["I don't know you"] is about relationship – not whether we are saved or not
2. Does Jesus know me?
3. Biblical Slavery: a) exclusive ownership; b) complete submission; c) singular devotion; d) total dependence.

Week 3 – We are **AVAILABLE** to God.

1. Why would God be working in my life: a) change me; b) impact others thru me; c) relationship between He and me.
2. Do I have a friend who would call me out if I am off track?
3. My relationship needs to be intentional.

Week 4 – We **SEEK** after God.

1. Ps 9:10 – He will never forsake those who seek Him.
2. Seeking is accomplished with serious intent and commitment – I am all in.
3. Ps 34

Week 5 – We **ABIDE** (spend time) with God.

1. Define: unbroken fellowship; constantly before me; continual
2. Jn 15:1-17 – Jesus is the Vine and I need to stay connected.
3. Goal of abiding is bearing fruit.

Week 6 – We **KNOW** God.

1. If want to boast about something, boast about knowing God.
2. "Knowing" implies intimate understanding.
3. Prove our knowledge thru action – we cannot confess with our lips and deny with our life.
4. "Knowing" implies we possess many of the other relational characteristics of a Jesus follower.

Week 7 – We **LOVE** God.

1. Agape is a decision, not an emotion.
2. We love God totally: heart, mind, body, and soul.
3. Love pervades all the fruit of the Spirit.

Week 8 – We **OBEY** God.

1. Obedience may be the basic relationship characteristic.
2. Disobedience can quickly destroy relationship.
3. Obedience does not produce love, but love produces obedience.
4. God may test our obedience.

Week 9 – We **TRUST** God.

1. Do I trust and depend on God or just intellectually confirm that trust. Trust means I do not depend on self.
2. Circumstances of life should not impact my faith/trust.

Week 10 – We walk **HUMBLY** with God.

1. Pride and arrogance are the enemies of humility.
2. One cannot be a true Christ follower without being humble, submissive, and surrendered to God.

Week 11 – We **ENJOY** God.

1. Joy comes from the knowledge of God, relationship, and His Word.
2. Trials and suffering should not impact our joy.
3. Key: Knowing I can do anything through Him who strengthens me.

Week 12 – We **WORSHIP** God.

1. Is my worship acceptable: (1) free from sin; (2) rooted in the Word, (3) focused on Christ; (4) coming from heart?

Appendix D
Relationship Life Plan

INTRODUCTION

You may be wondering after finishing this study, what to do next. When I first developed this study and the concepts of this book, I decided to develop an outline of a Life Plan that would be consistent with a goal of "being right with God."

You might find reviewing this abbreviated outline helpful as you consider your next steps.

GOALS
     (1) To be a faithful follower of Jesus,
     (2) To stay connected to Jesus,
     (3) To have genuine fellowship with Jesus, and
     (4) To grow in maturity with Jesus.

I concluded that I would fail if my goal was obedience.

RESPONSIBILITY

(1) I want an intimate love relationship with God through Christ!

(2) My life must be about relationships:

     a) being right with God,
     b) being right with one another, and
     c) being right with the world.

(3) My most critical relationship is with Christ and the key to this relationship is abiding (John 15:15).

RELATIONSHIP

The call on my life is not to performance or activity – it is to <u>follow</u> Him, to <u>know</u> Him, to <u>abide</u> in Him. It's all about relationship because He wants me to be with Him. The purpose of the relationship is to know God, and thus I must spend time with Him developing that relationship.

Everything God wants to do through me, He will accomplish out of the excess love that flows from my relationship with Him. The focus is on knowing and connection (relationship), not on activity or ministry.

If I confuse spiritual activity with spiritual maturity my Christian life will become exhausting. I simply cannot do enough to please God. There is too much guilt produced in not living up to God's standards or one's own expectations. My goal must be the relationship, not the activity that is produced from following Him .

OBEDIENCE

John 14:15 says that "If you love me, you will keep my commands." Unfortunately I tend to put the emphasis on the second half of that statement. Obedience will flow out of the love. If I love me more than I love God, my obedience to Christ will suffer in direct proportion to the weakness of my love for Him.

Obedience, although important as evidence of salvation, is not required to gain or maintain my salvation. I am saved by the blood of the Lamb once and for all.

***God's love for me will never change
regardless of what I do or don't do.***

Transformation Road Map

Primary Takeaways

1: God's love is unconditional and ever-present and we are called to imitate this love in our daily lives. By walking in love and imitating God we demonstrate our faith to others.

2: Our relationship with God should be characterized by reciprocating His unconditional love and actively demonstrating it in our daily lives in order to deepen our connection with Him and serve as living testimonies of our faith.

3: We make ourselves available to God and willingly responding to His call with trust and obedience, regardless of our perceived qualifications or skills. We have received a new identity in Christ and the blessings we've received should motivate us to live in a manner worthy of our calling.

4: Pursuing and seeking God should be an intentional, active, and earnest process, not a passive or rote acceptance of His calling. Diligently seeking God leads to finding Him, receiving His blessings, and experiencing success in our spiritual lives.

5: Abiding in God means we maintain a close, constant, and intimate relationship with Jesus, allowing His power to work through us and produce spiritual fruit. We should intentionally seek after Christ leading to demonstrating our love and obedience.

6: Knowing God is not a passive experience but an active and pursuit that involves intentionally seeking Him. This pursuit leads to a deeper, more intimate relationship with God and allows us to walk humbly with our God.

7: Obedience should be a natural desire to follow Christ's teachings, drawing us into deeper intimacy with Him. While struggling with disobedience is inevitable, a true follower of Christ will consistently desire and work to obey. We will feel convicted by the Holy Spirit when we disobey.

8: Trusting God is built upon knowing God's character and His Word. It is essential for developing an intimate and resilient relationship with Him. Trusting in God means we have an unwavering confidence and dependence on Him in all circumstances.

9: Enjoying God is integrated in all the experiences of our walk with God. True enjoyment stems from revering His holiness, obeying His commands, and gratefully acknowledging His benefits, leading to a life of delight in His presence and automatic alignment with His will.

10: Worshipping God is an essential principle of a Christian's faith walk. We are to offer praise, thanksgiving, and reverence to God, acknowledging His supremacy and goodness. This stems from a heart of love and obedience which is overflowing with love and compassion for others.

What are you being called to do next?

Leader Guide

This Guide is designed to give a leader answers and additional information to effectively lead a group discussion of each lesson in this book.

Tips For Leading
We recommend that you begin a group discussion by reading an appropriate Scripture. It may be one that you will cover in the material or another related passage you have chosen. This will do several things:

- Allow time for everyone to get settled.
- Remind everyone of the subject and bring their minds to a common focus.
- Provide a transition from the previous activity.

Additional ice-breakers are usually not necessary, but if your group is new or members don't know each other well, you could have someone give their testimony/story at the beginning of each week. If you sense that the group needs additional focus before you begin the discussion, conduct a short discussion about the themes of the lesson or ask about the meaning of a particular term associated with the lesson.

Goals
The discussion should center around the questions in the lesson. Remember that each person in your group has different goals and is at a different place in his or her Christian walk. Jesus may be an old friend to some but a new acquaintance to others. The dynamic of the group will vary depending on the nature of the participants.

Your goal as the Leader should be to foster understanding and familiarity with Scripture. For new believers or participants who are not comfortable with the Bible, your goal should be to help them get over that hurdle and begin to seek knowledge and understanding from His Word.

More mature participants will probably dig deeper to find personal meaning and understanding. They may particularly desire to discuss application questions and issues.

Prayer
Unless you have an outstanding person of prayer in your group, you as the leader should wrap up your discussion time with prayer that specifically reflects the discussion and the themes, purpose, and focus of the lesson.

Answers

Introduction
LEADER: Consider randomly passing out names to everyone in your group so each member has a name of one other person in the group that they will pray for during the time of this study.

Lesson 1 – Being Loved by God
Q1. Ans: (1) Bible says so; (2) His grace toward me; (3) He chose me; (4) Assurance, peace, rest; (5) answers to prayer; (6) transformed life.
Q2. What do you learn or observe in the following verses?
John 15:9 Jesus loves me just like God loves Jesus!
Deuteronomy 7:6-8 We are holy to God; He chose us; treasured possession (see next question)
Q3. Ans: Possession means that we are His. He created us and we belong to Him. "Treasure" implies something very valuable and desirable.
John 15:16 He chose me! And, He chose us in both the Old Testament (OT) and the New Testament (NT).
John 15:13 He gave His life; paid my sin debt.
Q5. He loves me; I am treasured; He proved it by dying for me.
Q6. Ans: <u>Nothing</u> can separate us from the love of God. LEADER: Ask the group: "But what about sin?"
Q7. Zephaniah 3:17 Ans: He is mighty and can save; He will delight and rejoice over me; quiet me with His love; rejoice or exult over me *with singing!*
Romans 5:8 Ans: While "still sinners", meaning I don't have to get clean first
Q8. Ans: None that I can think of. That's why it's <u>grace</u>. You did nothing to earn it or deserve it. God's love, mercy, and grace compelled Him to save us.
<u>Ephesians 2:4-5</u> Rich in mercy; alive with Christ (even as sinners); grace
Ephesians 3:19 We may know God's love and be filled with it. LEADER: You may want to ask, "What do you think this means?" Ans: (1) So great it cannot be fully known or understood by man; (2) God is infinite and eternal and we have access to His resources …. In this case His love
<u>1 John 3:1</u> We are children of God
<u>1 John 4:12</u> Ans: His love perfected in us. *"Perfected"* = Since our love has its source in God's love, His love, then, is made complete/perfect (or receives full expression) when we love others. Thus, the God "in us" that no one has seen, is seen in us, because He abides in us.

1 John 4:8-10 God is love; Jesus is our atoning sacrifice → Grace in love
Q10. 1. Jesus (Son) died for all
2. will graciously give us all things
3. we are justified
4. no one can condemn us
5. Jesus is interceding for us
Q11. Ans: gratitude; thanksgiving ; desire to serve; obey.
Q14. Ans: Those characteristics might include: humility; submission/surrender; gratitude. LEADER: You may get many different kinds of responses to this question – that's ok.
What I Want to Remember:
LEADER: Emphasize the importance of Lesson 2. Lesson 2 sets the tone and foundation for the entire study: *Relationship*

Lesson 2 – A Relationship with God
Q1. Mt 4:19 Called to be fishers of men.
Mt 16:24 Followers should deny themselves and take up their cross.
Jn 10:27-28 We listen to His voice; we are known by Him; He will give us eternal life; we are secure in Him.

Lesson 3 – Being Available to God
INTRODUCTION
Secular Definition of being "available"
- Easy or possible to use
- Present or ready for use
- Able or willing to be on hand
- Synonyms: accessible, attainable, obtainable

Q1. 2 Corinthians 5:1 If we are in Christ then we are a new creation.
2 Corinthians 3:18 We are being transformed into His likeness.
Ro 8:29 We are being transformed; Jesus is the first among many brothers.
Q2. It's a do-over! We are being transformed into the image of Christ by: Sanctification - Fruit of the Spirit - He is changing us - The key action words new and conformed say we are being changed.
Q3. 1 – We are apathetic or lazy. We may be old or tired.
2 – Stubborn: we want to do it ourselves – but we don't.
3 - I don't have a strong foundation in Christ.
4 - Weak relationship with the Divine.
5 - No Christian friends who care enough to call me out and set me straight!
Q4. Colossians 1:9-10 Live worthy using the knowledge of His will.
Phil 1:27 Walk worthy of the Gospel. . . standing firm. Striving for the faith.
Q5. If you say NO – we need His power, knowledge and wisdom, perfection, presence. If you say YES – we must self-sacrifice; have forgiving spirit; humility.
WILLING and AVAILABLE
Psalms 51:12-13 David asks God to give him a willing spirit so he can teach sinners God's ways.
Isa 1:18-20 Even though I am a sinner, if I am willing and obedient, I will be blessed.
Mk 14:38 We may want to, but we may have to fight the flesh to take action.
1 Peter 5:2-3 Serve God because you are willing, not because of bondage.

Q6. 1-Be prepared in advance.
2-Draw the line in advance – because the flesh is weak.
3-Be ready for trials.
The implication is that this sanctification process may not be easy!
Q7. He went immediately → So Abram left, as the Lord had told him." There was no delay or argument?
LEADER: You might ask the group why they think Abraham responded in this way (without hesitation). Let's assume there were many reasons unknown to us that caused Abraham to leave his home and travel to unknown places. Abraham made the right choice here and followed God's instructions.
Q8. 1. Joseph and Mary take Baby Jesus to Egypt.
2. The fishermen followed Jesus.
3. Ananias went and laid hands on Paul.
4. Zaccheous in tree – he was creative.
5. Isaiah – the ideal response.
6. Shadrach, Meshach and Abednego.
7. Jonah.
8. Hosea.
LEADER: You might ask your group if they can think of any other examples.

Lesson 4 – Pursuing and Seeking God
MEDITATION:
   LEADER - Note Lord's Response: hears; delivers; saves; protects; redeems
DEFINITIONS
Secular definitions of seeking or pursuing:
- to go in search of; to search out; to track down
- look for; to hunt; to chase after
- to try to discover;
- to try to acquire or gain; to strive after.

OBSERVATIONS
Acts 17:27 God <u>can</u> be found.
1 Chronicles 22:19 Set your mind (devote your heart and soul). This means to be committed, dedicated, and have compelling motives.
Zephaniah 2:3 Seek the character of God [here that is righteousness and humility]. We want His perfect character to be manifest in us. We want to imitate the nature of God.
Q2. Blessing and righteousness.
Righteousness implies we have been cleared, exonerated, and acquitted. How many of us want that! It is not enough to know about God, we must know Him personally, we need a relationship in order to be declared righteous. (a saving relationship)
Q3. Verse 4: Clean hands and a pure heart; not following false idols which are false and not practicing deceit.
LEADER: You might ask, "How important do you think this requirement is?"
Q4. My ultimate pursuit must be for heart knowledge, not head knowledge. It is the condition of my heart that must be changed and improved – then and only then will my soul thirst for God.
Q5. *Earnestly* I seek you; my *soul thirsts* for you, my body *longs* for you, . . .
LEADER: Have group explain what they think these terms mean.
Q6. We are to seek after Him with heart, mind, and soul – completely!

Q7. What benefits can you identify in the following verses?
2 Chronicles 26:3-5 Seeking brings God's blessing and success.
Psalms 9:10 God never forsakes. Forsake means to abandon, leave, renounce, turn away, or give up.
Psalms 34:4 God will respond => answered prayer.
Psalms 34:10 We will lack no good thing – provision
Proverbs 28:5 Understand justice
Q8. Possible Benefits: Answered me, delivered me, saved me, rescued me, I not lack for any good thing, protects me, redeems me, and does not punish me.

HOW TO SEEK GOD
Isaiah 55:6 Do it now!
Psalm 105:4 Do it always or continuously. It should be an attitude and lifestyle.
Q9. n/a
Q10. We are to pursue God constantly, continually, repeatedly, on every occasion, incessantly, and perpetually. This means that our thoughts are always (frequently, as often as possible) on the Lord.
Matthew 6:33 First or top priority.
Jeremiah 29:12-13 With all your heart.
Hebrews 11:6 He rewards those who sincerely seek Him.
Q11. 2 Chronicles 15:15 Whole desire or eagerly.
Seeking God eagerly means we do it thirstily, with keen interest, intense desire, and expectantly. The KJV translates eagerly as "with all the soul." This means a very strong overriding desire – I will not be defeated in my seeking. I look forward to connecting with God, anticipating a joyful and fulfilling result.
Q.12 The benefit is: rest all around.
It means: Rest from enemies is part of God's blessing for obedience in Chronicles (14:5-7, here and 1 Chron 22:8-9, 18. Righteous kings have victory and wicked rulers experience defeat. They are rewarded with rest because of their genuine repentance (Dt 4:29; 1 Sam 7:3)
Psalms 77:2 Persevere (without wearying).
We must persevere in prayer. We must not give up if the answers do not come immediately. We should seek the Lord until we find Him. We should not get tired and give up.
Psalms 40:16 With praise and worship.

THOUGHT OR DISCUSSION QUESTIONS
1. a. b. c. **LEADER:** In your group, list the "things" on a board, if possible. Then have the class choose the best three.
Ans: a <u>heart</u> exercise, intentional, relentless, earnest, diligent.

Lesson 5 – Abiding in God
THE SCENE (John 15)
Secular definition of "abide":
- to wait for or await
- to stay or live somewhere
- to remain or continue
- to accept without objection
- SYN: stay, dwell, hang around, remain

HOW DO WE ABIDE?

Are you right with God?

1 John 2:9 Do not hate your brother, rather *love* your brother.
1 John 4:12 Love one another.
1 John 4:16 Live in *love*.
John 15:9-10 Obey commands + remain in *love*.

Q1. LOVE. It appears that the overall characteristic in these Scriptures indicates I am walking as Jesus would want me to – I am following his commands, His teaching, His desire for my life. I am not outside His will rebelling against how He wishes me to live. Thus, I am living in obedience, loving God, and loving my brother. I obey and love!

Q3. The relationship is unbroken. Unbroken would mean: constantly present, constant influence, and continually operative. In John 15, the abiding refers to holding onto the Vine, thus maintaining unbroken fellowship.

Q4. Spending time together.

SPEND TIME WITH GOD LEADER: Ask, "What does this mean to you?" Obviously the requirement for bearing fruit is abiding.

Q5. Ans. "Apart from me you can do nothing." It does not literally mean nothing, but nothing of eternal value or significance.

Q6. What are the three commands in the above passage:
1. Abide in Me.
2. Abide in My love.
3. Love one another as I have love you.

In order to bear fruit we must "abide." And, in order to abide in His love we must keep His commands (obey).

Q7. Ans. "As I have loved you." This means it is pure unselfish love (agape), like defined in 1 Cor 13.

OBEY: John 15:10 Just as I obeyed my Father's commands
LOVE: John 15:12 As I have loved you.

Q8. Ans: OBEY: I should obey Jesus' commands and I should love others as Jesus loved me. And, since Jesus would never fail, if we are to do as He did, then we will not fail.

Q9. Ans: A relationship and the power of God, or spending quality time with God. One can truly obey, but only if a relationship exists.

WALKING IN THE SPIRIT (Romans 8:1-17)
8:1 No condemnation in Christ Jesus.
8:2 The law of Spirit set me free from law of sin and death.
8:9 We are controlled by the Spirit, not sinful nature.
8:17 We are heirs of God and co-heirs with Christ.

Q10.
Hebrews 3:1 Fix your thoughts on Jesus.
Philippians 4:8 Think about such things as whatever is true, noble, right, pure, lovely, admirable, excellent or praiseworthy.
Romans 12:3 Do not think of yourself more highly than you ought.
Ephesians 4:23 Be made new in the attitude of your minds.
1 Peter 1:13 Prepare your minds for action.

Q11.
- So we will concentrate on the "right" things (things of God).
- So mind and heart in harmony.
- If mind distracted, heart will be overridden.
- In order that Holy Spirit can influence us.
- Concepts must go through the filter of the mind to get to the heart.

Lesson 6 – Knowing God

MEDITATION
LEADER: You might ask your group: "Did anyone have a revelation this week while you were meditating on this passage?" Note that "This" is referring to: (1) faith growing abundantly, (2) love for each other increasing, (3) steadfastness in faith in your persecutions and afflictions.

KNOWING GOD
Secular definitions: "knowing"
- to have information or understanding about someone
- to understand or have clear idea about something
- SYN: comprehend; grasp; understand

A JESUS FOLLOWER KNOWS GOD
1 John 5:20 To know Christ means we know God.
1 John 4:8 To know God, one must *love God and brothers.*
John 17:3 Knowing God means *eternal life.*
2 Peter 1:3 Through knowledge of Him we get divine power to live godly.

Q1. To know Him:
a) have power of His resurrection
b) have fellowship with Him in His sufferings
c) being conformed to His image (like Him in death)
d) thus, because of these things I press on

Q2. John 14:17 Evidence that you know Him – He abides with you (indwells).
Q3. Knowing means I <u>know</u> God! Salvation goes hand-in-hand with knowing.

OBSERVATIONS FROM 1 JOHN – Lesson 6
1 John 2:3 Obey Him.
1 John 2:6 Walk as Jesus did.
1 John 4:21 Love Him and love one another).
1 John 4:7-8 *Beloved, let us <u>love one another</u>, for love is from God, and whoever loves has been born of God and <u>knows God</u>. 8 Anyone who does not love does not know God, because God is love.* ESV

Q4. By demonstrating or practicing obedience.
Explanation: If we know God we will experience the benefits of a relationship with Him; for example, the fruit of the Spirit will become more and more evident in our lives, particularly as we follow His ways.

Q5. God delights in kindness and love, justice, and righteousness <u>on earth</u>. Knowing God is more important or valuable than wisdom or strength or wealth.

Q6. Because we are to <u>truly</u> to know God – it cannot be a superficial knowing.
Q7. Titus 1:16 Good deeds show we know Him.
1 Jn 4:8 Love shows we know Him (see also 1 Cor 8:1-3).
1 Jn 3:6 No continual sin.
Jer 22:16 Plead the cause of the needy.

Q8. a) Knowing God means we love others, not just relate to God.
b) Knowing spills over to loving others.
c) Knowing God empowers us to do other things, particularly good deeds.

Q9. Entrance to Kingdom is denied – not knowing implies there is no relationship and no relationship means there is no saving faith.

Q10. LEADER: You might list on board all the <u>general</u> things that are hindrances based on the input from your group. You might then ask, " What

would lessen the distractions or make them go away?"
Q11. n/a

Lesson 7 – Loving God
MEDITATION - LEADER: Ask your group what revelations they might have received during their meditation during the week.
Q1. How do we love God with our HEART – SOUL – MIND - STRENGTH?
HEART: See the Psalms of David, written with passion and feeling!
SOUL: [Philip Doddridge PRAYER on "not my will, but yours be done"
From "*Loving God from the SOUL*"]
"This day do I, with the utmost solemnity, surrender myself to thee. I renounce all former lords that have had dominion over me; and I consecrate to thee all that I am, and all that I have; the faculties of my mind, the members of my body, my worldly possessions, my time, and my influence over others; to be all used entirely for thy glory, and resolutely employed in obedience to thy commands, as long as thou continues me in life . . . To thee I leave the management of all events, and say without reserve, "Not my will, but thine be done."
MIND: Philippians 4:8 *Finally brothers, whatever is true, whatever is honorable, whatever is just, whatever is pure, whatever is lovely, whatever is commendable—if there is any moral excellence and if there is any praise— dwell on these things.*(HCSB)
Isaiah 26:3 *You will keep in perfect peace the mind that is dependent on You, for it is trusting in You.* (HCSB)
STRENGTH: John 15:5 "I am the vine; you are the branches. The one who remains in Me and I in him produces much fruit, because you can do nothing without Me.
2 Corinthians 12:9-10 But He said to me, "My grace is sufficient for you, for power is perfected in weakness." Therefore, I will most gladly boast all the more about my weaknesses, so that Christ's power may reside in me. 10 So because of Christ, I am pleased in weaknesses, in insults, in catastrophes, in persecutions, and in pressures. For when I am weak, then I am strong. HCSB
Q2. Seems all inclusive! I need His help to love Him in this way.
OBSERVATIONS: John 13:34-35 As I loved you – love others
Q3a. Because God is love. (1 John 4:8, 16)
Q3b.
John 14:15, 24 If you love, then you keep His commands.
John 15:10, 12, 17 Love each other.
Q4. "as I have loved you" Do any of us think we are capable of loving like Jesus?
Q5. To be a child of God means to love your brother. If we do not love, the alternative is death. The meaning is that a true believe will love God and love one another. If a person is not or can't do that, then they are not children of God, unsaved, and life eternally separated from God will continue to be their future. They are "dead" relative to God.
1 John 2:15 Do not love the world.
1 John 3:18 Love in deeds, not talk. Jesus wants action, good deeds, etc.
1 John 4:7-8 Love comes from God; if you love then you know God.
1 John 4:18-20 We cannot love God if we do not love our brother.

Q6. 1 John 5:2-3 *By this we know that we love the children of God, when we love God and obey his commandments. 3 For this is the love of God, that we keep his commandments. And his commandments are not burdensome.* ESV

Q7. It would be reasonable to conclude this from the two following passages: (1) Mt 22:37-39 Jesus said: "'Love the Lord your God with all your heart and with all your soul and with all your mind.' This is the first and greatest commandment. And the second is like it: 'Love your neighbor as yourself.' NIV (2) Matt 10:37 "Anyone who loves his father or mother more than me is not worthy of me; anyone who loves his son or daughter more than me is not worthy of me. NIV

Q8. The Bible says that God <u>is</u> love. Love is likely spread throughout all of God's attributes. When God does anything it is likely filtered through love.

THE FRUIT OF THE SPIRIT: Love is kind

Love is kind, it does not envy, it does not boast

Love is not proud, it is not rude

Love is not easily angered

Love does not delight [rejoice] but rejoices

Love is patient

Love always perseveres

Love always trusts, always hopes

Q9. Love Is the ultimate attribute of God. **LEADER:** You might ask, "If it is true that love is the ultimate attribute of God, then what are the implications of that fact?

SUMMARY/CONCLUSION

And above all these put on love, which binds everything together in perfect harmony. (ESV) **LEADER:** Ask your class what they think this means. How would they explain this to a new believer?

Lesson 8 – Obeying God

LEADER: You might open the week's discussion asking about a popular hymn! Find a copy of "Trust and Obey" in a hymnal and ask your group to answer the following questions:

Q. Verse 1: What are we to do? (1) walk with Lord; (2) by light of His Word; (3) do His good will

Q. What does God do? (1) sheds glory on our way (2) He abides

Q. Verse 3: What does God do when we trust & obey? (1) Favor; (2) Joy

Q. What are we to do other than trust & obey? Lay all on the alter

Q. Verse 4: If we trust & obey, what do we do? (1) Fellowship; (2) Sit at His feet; (3) Walk by His side

Q. Based on the chorus, what is it we get if we trust & obey? *Happy in Jesus*

MEDITATION

Solomon came to this conclusion after looking back over his life and recognizing that for life not to be meaningless it had to include God, and be <u>lived in a life of obedience</u>. Again "the fear of the Lord" is linked closely with obedience. Remember, Solomon was considered one of the wisest people to ever live – he wrote most of Proverbs.

MEANING OF OBEDIENCE

Secular definition of obedience:
- to do what the law or someone tells you to do
- to follow the commands or guidance of another

Are you right with God?

- to conform or comply

Q1. LEADER: Ask: If you ignore any religious connection when you think of obedience, is it negative or positive?

Q2. Ans: If I am a true Christ follower, then I will obey – that must inherently be the case. But that does not mean that I always obey or that I must obey or lose my salvation or standing with God. But continued or willful disobedience can mean separation from God. We become separated from our relationship with Him and are not in fellowship.

IMPORTANCE OF OBEDIENCE

1) Partial
2) chosen
3) knowing
4) model or example
5) teach

Q3. NOTE: It is not to teach the rules, it is teach to obey the rules. We do that by example, like Jesus did (John 15:10).

LEADER: Mt 19:17 may be raised in your group about the requirement of obedience related to salvation: *And he said to him, "Why do you ask me about what is good? There is only one who is good. If you would enter life, keep the commandments."* ESV

NOTE: Jesus said this when Israel was still under the Law. The people did not yet know or understand being saved by faith alone in Jesus.

Q5. Love is demonstrated by obedience. Obedience comes from loving Christ.

LEADER: You might ask your group what they think that conclusion means to them personally.

THE CRITICAL NATURE OF OBEDIENCE

Acts 13:22 God considered David a man after his own heart, because God knew David would obey. He would "do all my will." Or "do everything I want him to do."

Jn 15:14 Those Christ considered friends were obedient.

> **Q6.** Abraham and Moses (2 Chron 20:7 and Ex 33:11)
> **LEADER:** You might ask your group, "Why were Abraham and Moses considered friends of God?"

Dt 6:2 and Ps 103:17-18 Obedience is linked with the fear of the Lord in both passages. **LEADER:** Ask: "What is the "fear" referenced here?

> Ans: Reverence; obedience; worship

It would also imply that verse is directed at true followers.

> **Q7.** Ans: Here "life" is linked to "the fear of the Lord" and in the above obedience is also linked to "fear."

Act 5:27-29 ans Jn 14:21,31: Obedience to Christ/God is more important than manmade rules or laws. **LEADER:** You may want to ask, "What are some of the rules of some cults – rules made by men?"

> (1) must confess to a priest; (2) must worship on Saturday; (3) must believe in Pre-trib rapture; (4) must speak in tongues. 5) (a) Jesus promised that He would reveal Himself to those who obey. (b) Father will love him.

Q8. God will test our obedience, For example: Judges 2:22 *in order to test Israel by them, whether they will take care to walk in the way of the Lord as their fathers did, or not.* ESV

Q9. LEADER: You may want to ask, "Does God still test people today?" **YES!**

Q10. 1 John 3:22 Receive answers to prayer
Luke 11:28 Blessed.
Acts 5:32 Empower: Indwelling and filling of the Holy Spirit.
Matthew 12:50 Part of the Family of God – Salvation (see also Heb 5:9).
Romans 6:16 Leads to righteousness → salvation.
Q12. YES and NO.
If YES: You must obey the designated way to be saved.
If NO: Strict Obedience is not required to maintain your salvation.
It does *prove* your salvation.
Q13. Ans: Knowing God/Jesus is a matter of life and death for everyone, whether they know it or not. We must be diligent in having gospel conversations with the lost.
SUMMARY/CONCLUSION
LEADER: What does "ignorance" mean in this context?
Ans: It does NOT mean dumb, but rather without knowledge of God.

Lesson 9 – Depend on and Trust God

NOTE TO LEADER: The focus is on depending and trusting God – not on the sense that trust = faith. The question is: Do I trust God, not do I trust in God.
MEDITATION
Idols are lifeless and have no power. God is our help and shield.
DEFINITIONS
Secular definition of trust:
- belief someone is reliable, good, honest, or effective, etc.
- assured reliance on ability, strength, or truth of someone
- to depend or place confidence in someone
- SYN: confidence, credence, faith

WHAT DOES TRUSTING GOD MEAN?
Psalms 20:7 Implication: Not trusting in our own strength/abilities.
Proverbs 3:5 Not trusting in your own ways, skills, knowledge or self. See also Ps 20:7 above. Do it with all your heart – in faith not on your own understanding. Trusting God means *obeying his commands even when we don't fully understand*.
Psalms 37:5 Trust implies one will or must commit, if there is trust.
Q2. Definition of "commit": to decide to use; to definitely agree to do something; to make yourself obligated for something; a pledge of support or to act.
Ps 56:3-4 I will not be afraid and become tentative. What can man do to me?
Isaiah 8:17 Wait on the Lord → be patient.
John 14:1 *Don't worry* about anything, just like Jesus advises in Mt 6:25-34.
Philippians 1:6 God is faithful so I can be confident.

Summarize the key thoughts in the above verses.
Ps 20:7 Don't trust in your own strength.
Pr 3:5 Trust with all your heart.
Ps 37:5 If I commit, He will act.
Ps 56: 3-4 Don't be afraid.
Isa 8:17 Be patient.
John 14:1 Don't worry or be anxious.
Phil 1:6 Have confidence.

Q3. To be unfaithful would be contrary to His basic nature (unchanging; perfect). But, what if we are unfaithful? 2 Timothy 2:13 *if we are faithless, he remains faithful—for he cannot deny himself.* ESV

Q4. Ans: Strong foundation of knowledge; strong relationship; high degree of faith; spiritual maturity; experience God in life fulfilling needs.

Q5. Gen 6:5-22 In faith Noah built boat.
Gen 22: 1-12 Abraham willing to sacrifice Isaac.
1 Sam 17:45-47 David and Goliath.
Daniel 6:23 Daniel in Lion's Den.

Q6. It means recognizing that God is trustworthy and then *trusting him regardless* of the circumstances. Note: Noah worked on the Ark for 100+ years. Daniel was saved from the lions because he was found blameless. Abraham had such faith in God that he took Isaac to be sacrificed. David knew God was with him.

WHAT HAPPENS WHEN WE TRUST?
Psalms 9:10 God has never forsaken those who seek/trust Him.

Q7. Ans: (1) know your name; (2) seeking God.
Psalms 37:5-6 God will make your righteousness shine.
Isaiah 26:3 You are at perfect peace.

Q8. We are focused on God.
Jeremiah 39:18 God can save you from physical death.
Romans 15:13 You will be filled with joy, peace, and hope.

Q10. God may not rescue me, but that does not impact my faith! I will not break important commands of God, just to save my physical life. Difficulties, struggles and trials should not impact my faith or trust in God.

LEADER: Ask the following question: "Do you feel this way? Would you give up your life rather than break one of God's commmands? Why? Why not?"

SUMMARY/CONCLUSION
What you do that demonstrates you don't really trust God:
(1) Save wealth (in excess of real needs and reasonable buffer)
(2) Don't tithe.
(3) To find job.
(4) To provide.
(5) Protect from evil.
(6) To find a spouse.

Numbers 23:19 *God is not man, that he should lie, or a son of man, that he should change his mind. Has he said, and will he not do it? Or has he spoken, and will he not fulfill it?* ESV

Lesson 10 – Walk Humbly With Your God
MEDITATION
In Mt 18:3-4 we have a rather definitive statement relative to our salvation. If we do not humble ourselves before a mighty God we will "never enter the kingdom of heaven." Is that statement shocking? This passage says our own interests are no longer paramount, but the interests of others should be a priority. Our attitude toward God must be like that of a little child who totally relies on and trusts in his earthly father. Jesus describes in 18:4 what He means in 18:3 by stating He means that by becoming like a little child means we must humble ourselves.

DEFINITIONS Being humble means I do not demand my way, I depend on God. Humility does <u>not</u> desire or encourage the notice of others. Rather, it means I observe and respond to the needs of others. The underlying problem: I am proud! I am focused on self, rather than God and others.

Q1. Ans: Even though you may think following Jesus might be hard, difficult, or demanding, take heart because it is not that severe and the pay-off is big: "rest for your soul."

Q2. Ans: Demanding, testing, arduous . . . impossible! More like a loving dictator.

HUMILITY TOWARD GOD

Philippians 2:8 Obedience to God's will – Jesus humbled Himself by taking on the nature of a servant and human likeness.

Q3. All thru the gospels Jesus said He did only what the Father wanted him to do and said only what the Father asked Him to say. Jesus washed the disciples' feet. The Incarnation is described as Jesus humbling Himself (Php 2)

Romans 12:3 Sober thinking – Don't think more highly of yourself.

Q4. Ans: Serious, truthful, thoughtful, and earnest consideration.

HUMILITY TOWARD ONE ANOTHER

Luke 14:10-11 Allowing others to be honored. Not seeking to be exalted.
Hebrews 13:17 Submitting to spiritual leaders – they are accountable to God.
1 Peter 5:5 Being subject to one another – listen to and serve one another.
Matthew 5:38-39 Accepting humiliation. Offenses will come: how will we react.

SUMMARY

Micah 6:8 Humility is a clear requirement in the OT.

Q5. The requirements are: being just, loving kindness, and walking humbly with God. It certainly could be argued that a broad definition of these three characteristics covers a great deal of territory that might be nearly adequate, particularly in a works-based religious environment as existed under the Old Covenant in those days. Today, under the New Covenant the focus changes and the salvation requirements are different, but justice, loving kindness, and walking humbly with God still cover a lot of territory.

Ephesians 4:1-2 Likewise in the NT, but here the requirements are: humility, gentleness, patience, and bearing with one another.

Q6. Malachi 4:1 Arrogance results in *judgment*.
2 Chronicles 32:25 Pride produced *wrath* and judgment from the Lord.
Proverbs 16:18 Pride causes destruction – it's just a matter of time.
Proverbs 6:16-17 The Lord hates pride (haughty eyes).

Q7. Ans: Pride will produce destruction, judgment . . . even wrath.

Q8. Ans: No . . . It appears to be almost required by definition.

Q9. Isaiah 66:2 Esteem

Proverbs 3:34 Grace

Psalms 147:6 Lifts us = Sustain

Psalms 25:9 Guide and teach.

Luke 18:14 Exalted

DISCUSSION AND THOUGHT QUESTIONS

3. Ans: (1) Recognize sinful nature; (2) Understands cannot measure up to God's standards on their own, (3) Overwhelmed by God's love and grace.

Are you right with God?

Lesson 11 – Enjoy God
MEDITATION
LEADER: Ask: Relative to the meditation passage this week, what does it mean or imply that our "joy may be full or complete"?
Our joy is dependent upon intimacy with Jesus and obedience to His word. Lack of joy is a love problem, not an obedience problem. If I am in Christ, then I will be abiding, which will result in fruit. This occurs because I am living in obedience

REJOICE & DELIGHT IN THE LORD
1 Chronicles 16:10 Rejoicing is for those who seek the Lord.
Psalms 16:11 The joy (pleasures) are eternal (forevermore).
Psalms 32:11 The gladness is for the righteous and upright.
Psalms 37:4 He will give joy if we delight.
Philippians 4:4 Always! The joy is there continually!
Q1. Jesus Follower:
1. Walking worthy and dealing with my sinful nature
2. Persevering in my faith (Heb 10:35-37)
3. Meeting responsibilities as a Jesus follower: (a) standing firm; (b) avoiding temptation; (c) being an overcomer
Non-Believers: salvation

PEACE
John 14:27 Do not be *troubled* or *afraid*.
Philippians 4:6-7 Pray. The Peace of God will guard our hearts.
Gentleness = Christ-like consideration of others.
LEADER: NOTE progression of rejoice, don't worry, and peace in Php 4:4-7.
Q3. Ans: This Scripture says you can't answer this question because it surpasses all understanding. ☺
Q5. 1. Authentic praise.
2. True intimate worship.
3. Thanksgiving (attitude of gratitude).
4. Contentment (no worry; not anxious).
5. Calm assurance; serenity; peace.
6. Confidence – I understand my God, my faith, and who I am relative to God; I have no concern about the future.
All of this because I have a right relationship with God.
Q6. Secular: I know I have the knowledge or skills to accomplish some task.
Biblical: I believe in the absolute truth and promises of Scripture and in the Gospel.
What do we learn from Hebrews relative to that confidence?
Hebrews 4:15-16 Jesus can sympathize and the result is mercy and grace.
Hebrews 10:35-36 Confidence will be rewarded; we need to persevere.
1 Jn 5:14-15 This is the confidence we have in approaching God: that if we ask anything according to his will, he hears us. 15 And if we know that he hears us — whatever we ask — we know that we have what we asked of him. [see also 1 Jn 3:21-22]
Hebrews 13:6 I can have confidence because of my helper – do not fear life.
Q7. We are visitors on this earth because we are citizens of heaven. This life is not our home. What man might do to us has no eternal significance.
Q8. See Heb 13:6 above and Php 4:12 below.
LEADER: It might be interesting to brainstorm a list on the board without

discussing. Then ask which ones are the most interesting, and why?
Q9. Ans: Our only real accomplishment is to know God/Christ. Nothing else ultimately matters.
Q10. I can do everything through him who gives me strength. **LEADER:** Ask, "Do you believe that?" At an appropriate time you might insert, "Prove it."
Q11. LEADER: Ask your group if someone has a testimony about being strengthened by God. It is often said that God equips those He sends. Has anyone in your group experienced that equipping?
1 Peter 1:3 LEADER: Ask your group what this means?
Q12. n/a
Q13. What is the object of our hope in the following passages?
Titus 3:7 Eternal life.
1 Thessalonians 5:8 Salvation.
Galatians 5:5 Righteousness.
Acts 23:6 Resurrection from the dead.
PERSONAL REFLECTION
1. Ans: Jesus followers must feel joy in knowing they are citizens of Heaven – just passing through this earthly life. The focus of our lives should be on relationship with God and not worldly success or values.
2. Ans: Less or no real worry vs. no purpose in life.
3. Stress; sin; suffering (me or others); life gets in the way.
SUMMARY/CONCLUSION
LEADER: You might ask before you end your discussion period, "What is the key to joy? Ans: (1) confidence in His Word; (2) relationship.

Lesson 12 – Worship God
MEDITATION
16:23 He brought us salvation.
16:24 Glory, His deeds.
16:25 He is great, worthy, to be feared.
16:26 He made (created) the heavens.
16:27 He is majestic, strength, joy.
16:28 Glory, strength.
16:29 Glory, bring offering, holiness.
16:30 World firmly established.
ACCEPTABLE WORSHIP
Heb 12:28-29 *We must worship acceptably and* do it with reverence and awe.
Malachi 1:8 Inferior: God wants only our best.
Matthew 15:9 In vain – following the rules of men.
John 4:22 *Ignorant* – we know not what we are doing.
Romans 1:22-23 Improper – idolatrous.
LEADER: Your group may need help in understanding these concepts.
Q3. Leviticus 9:7 The *first* thing I must do in approaching a holy God is to be free of sin. ALSO: Heb 10:4, because it is impossible for the blood of bulls and goats to take away sins . . . 10 And by that will, we have been made holy through the sacrifice of the body of Jesus Christ once for all.
Psalms 24:3-4 Like the OT priest, I must approach God in worship with clean hands and pure heart.

Are you right with God?

Note Exodus 30:20 Whenever they enter the Tent of Meeting, they shall wash with water so that they will not die. Also, when they approach the altar to minister by presenting an offering...

John 10:9 We must come to worship God through <u>Christ</u>.

Our focus MUST be on what the OT tabernacle foreshadowed – Christ.

Romans 12:1 My entire life is an act of worship.

John 6:35 Worship must be rooted in the Word.

ALSO: Eph 5:26 to make her holy, cleansing her by the washing with water through the word.

Mark 12:30 Our worship must be a matter of the <u>heart.</u>

Isaiah 1:12ff *When you come to appear before me, who has asked this of you, this trampling of my courts? 13 Stop bringing meaningless offerings! Your incense is detestable to me. . . . I cannot bear your evil assemblies. . . .*

Q4. 1. We must confess sin and ask forgiveness. We must be free from sin.
2. We should pray that the Word would cleanse and teach us. Worship is rooted in the Word.
3. Only approach the one true God through Christ – Christ must be the focus and the avenue.
4. Worship must involve both our hearts and mind. Worship comes from the heart.

Q5. Psalms 75:1 For the nearness of God's presence.

Psalms 106:1 For the goodness and mercy of God – love endures forever.

2 Corinthians 9:14-15 For the gift of Christ.

Romans 7:24-25 For deliverance from indwelling sin, through Christ.

1 Corinthians 15:56-57 For victory over death.

Q6. 1) His love endures forever.
   2) Christ's obedience; my deliverance.

LEADER: The gifts in the five passages are:
1. Nearness of God.
2A. Goodness and mercy of God.
2B. His love is forever.
3. Christ Jesus is our Savior.
4. We are delivered from sin.
5A. Victory over sin.
5B. God's grace.

PSALM 95:1-7
95:1-3 Sing, shout, come with thanksgiving, extol with music.
95:4 The Lord is great – above all Gods.
95:6B Bow down; kneel.

PSALMS 96:1-9
96:1-3 Sing, proclaim His salvation, declare His deeds.
96:4-6 He is great; Worthy of praise; Lord made Heavens; Splendor & majesty; strength.
96:7-8 Glory.
96:9 holiness – tremble.

Psalms 98:1-5
98:1 Sing.
98:1-3 Salvation.
98:4-5 Shout for joy; song; music with harp; singing; trumpets, horn.

Psalms 99:1-5

99:2:   He is great.
99:4   He is mighty, loves justice, established equity; just and right.
99:3, 5 He is holy.

Psalms 100
100:1   Shout.
100:2   With gladness; with joyful songs.
100:3   Yahweh is God; He is Creator; we are His people; He is our shepherd.
100:4   With thanksgiving; with praise.
100:5   He is good; loves endures forever; faithfulness.
        Why: 98:1-3   salvation
        Why: 98:9   judge in righteousness; equity

Q7. Loud, active, expressive; enthusiastic,
1) We learn a number of His attributes, His nature.
2) We learn that He desires worship, and that the worship desired appears to be very <u>active and expressive</u>.
3) He has provided us salvation, but He is also going to judge us

SUMMARY/CONCLUSION
LEADER: Here are several questions about you may want to discuss with your group.
Q. Do you believe the first sentence? . . . . "That worship is the ultimate goal of the church."
Q. If that is true, what are the implications?
Q. Do you think the last sentence above ["*For God is most reflected in us when we are most delighted in Him.*"] is true?

John Piper has written, "Missions is not the ultimate goal of the church. Worship is. Missions exist because worship doesn't. Worship is ultimate, not missions, because God is ultimate, not man. When this age is over, and the countless millions of the redeemed fall on their faces before the throne of God, missions will be no more. It is a temporary necessity. Bit worship abides forever"

Are you right with God?

Free PDF
MAKE WISE DECISIONS

[Get the ebook version for 99 cents]

Consequences Shape Lives.

This book discusses the nature of decisions and explores eight essential questions to make better decisions.

You are a few decisions away from transforming your life. You can make better decisions! This resource has sections on what makes a poor decision, questions to ask yourself, traps to avoid, short and sweet decisions, the wise decision framework, and twenty ways to be wise. It also has a handy decision-making checklist. (12 pages)

Free PDF: https://getwisdompublishing.com/resource-registration/

Kindle ebook for 99 cents: https://www.amazon.com/dp/B0FG8NC53J

Ebook

Free PDF

Ten Steps to Wise Choices

Timeless Wisdom. Practical Tools. Lasting Impact.

Are you right with God?

Free PDF
Life Improvement Principles
[Get the ebook version for 99 cents]

You can live your best life!

Welcome to a journey of discovery! In case you have forgotten, your actions have consequences. Unlock your potential! This book (60+ pages) provides the overview of all our strategies and wisdom principles to live your best life. You *can* transform your life! Get your wisdom-based roadmap to a better life and unlock all the possibilities for growth and success.

Free PDF: https://getwisdompublishing.com/resource-registration/

Kindle ebook for 99 cents:
https://www.amazon.com/dp/B0FG883KZM

Ebook

Free PDF

Make it your life goal to be the best you can be!

Discover Wisdom and live the life you deserve.

Are you right with God?

What Next?
Continue Your Journey

Continue Study in the *Jesus Follower* Series
The Jesus Follower Bible Study Series
https://www.amazon.com/dp/B0DHP39P5J

Be Challenged by the *OBSCURE* Series
The *OBSCURE* Bible Study Series
https://www.amazon.com/dp/B08T7TL1B1

Tackle Wisdom-Driven Life Change
Apply Biblical Wisdom to Live Your Best Life!
"Effective Life Change"
https://www.amazon.com/dp/1952359732

Know What You Should Pray
Personal Daily Prayer Guide
https://www.amazon.com/What-Should-Pray-Personal-Journal/dp/1952359260/

Decide to be the Very Best You Can Be
The Life Planning Series
https://www.amazon.com/dp/B09TH9SYC4

You Can Help:
SOCIAL MEDIA: Mention The Jesus Follower Bible Study Series on your social platforms. Include the hashtag #jesusbiblestudy so we are aware of your post.

FRIENDS: Recommend this series to your family, friends, small group, Sunday School class leaders, or your church.

REVIEW: Please give us your honest review at
https://www.amazon.com/dp/1952359589

Are you right with God?

The OBSCURE Bible Study Series

Continue your journey through the hidden
wisdom of Scripture with the OBSCURE Series.

  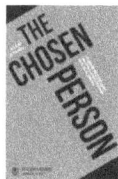 

Blasphemy, Grace, Quarrels & Reconciliation: The lives of first-century disciples.
This book presents Joseph of Arimathea, Joanna, Ananias, Hymenaeus, and Cornelius (a centurion). It illustrates the nature and challenges of life as a first-century disciple.

The Beginning and the End: From creation to eternity.
This book has four lessons from Genesis and four from Revelation covering creation, rebellion, grace, worship, and eternity. God is leading us to worship in the Throne Room.

God at the Center: He is sovereign and I am not.
This book examines the virgin birth, worship, prayer, the sovereignty of God, compromise, and trust. God is at the center of all these stories. He is at the center of our lives.

Women of Courage: God did some serious business with these women.
This book examines the lives of Jael, Rizpah, the woman of Tekoa, Tabitha, Shiphrah, and Lydia. These women exhibit great courage and faithfulness. God used them in amazing ways.

The Beginning of Wisdom: Your personal character counts.
In this book we find courage, loyalty, thankfulness, love, forgiveness, and humility. Personal character counts. Decisions have consequences. Wisdom will help us stand firm in our faith.

Miracles & Rebellion: The good, the bad, and the indifferent.
God hates sin and loves to heal the faithful. The rebellion of Korah, Haman, and Alexander compare to the healing stories of Aeneas, a slave girl, and the crippled man at Lystra.

The Chosen People: There is a remnant.
This book concentrates mostly on Israel in the Old Testament, but also covers some interesting subjects as Lucifer, Michael the archangel, and Job's wife.

The Chosen Person: Keep your eyes on Jesus.
The focus is on Jesus and the superiority of Christ. We investigate Melchizedek, the disciples on the road to Emmaus, Nicodemus, and the criminal on the cross.

WEBSITE: http://getwisdompublishing.com/products/
AMAZON: www.amazon.com/author/stephenhberkey

Are you right with God?

Life Planning Series

Read these books if you want to live a better life.

The primary audience for this series is the secular self-help market, but the concepts are Christian based.

	For the spiritual seeker and those with spiritual questions. *Your Spiritual Guidebook For Questions About Religion, God, Heaven, Truth, Evil, and the Afterlife.* https://www.amazon.com/dp/1952359473
	Core values will drive your life. https://www.amazon.com/dp/195235949X

Other Titles in the Life Planning Series
CHOOSE Integrity
CHOOSE Friends Wisely
CHOOSE The Right Words
CHOOSE Good Work Habits
CHOOSE Financial Responsibility
CHOOSE A Positive Self-Image
CHOOSE Leadership
CHOOSE Love and Family
LIFE PLANNING HANDBOOK A Life Plan Is The Key To Personal Growth https://www.amazon.com/gp/product/1952359325

Go to:

https://www.amazon.com/dp/B09TH9SYC4

to get your copy.

Are you right with God?

Personal Daily Prayer Guide
Prayer Resource and Journal

This is a great resource to kick-start your prayer life!

Know what to pray.
Pray based on Bible verses.
Strengthen your prayer life.
Access reference resources.
Pray with eternal implications.
Write your own prayers if desired.
Organize and focus your prayer time.
Learn what the Bible says about prayer.
Find encouragement and advice on how to pray.
Reduce frustration and distraction in your prayer time.

Get your copy today!

https://www.amazon.com/What-Should-Pray-Personal-Journal/dp/1952359260/

Acknowledgments

My wife has patiently persevered while I indulged my interest in writing. Thank you for all your help and assistance.

Our older daughter has been an invaluable resource. She has also graciously produced our website at www.getwisdompublishing.com

Our middle daughter designed the covers for most of my books, but I gave her a vacation on this Series. We are very grateful for her help, talent and creativity.

Notes

1 *agape,* Nelson's Illustrated Bible Dictionary.

2 Source unknown.

3 The Secrets of the Vine, Bruce Wilkinson, Pub. Global Vision Resources, copyright 2002, ISBN 97815905200307.

4 *abide*, Wuest's Word Studies.

5 Summarized from *The Life of a Jesus Follower*, Devotional Guide. Copyright 2004, 2007 by Hope Baptist Church, Las Vegas, Nevada, Written and published by church staff, Day 15.

About the Author

Steve attended church as a child and accepted Christ when he was 10 years old. But his walk with Jesus left a lot to be desired for the next 44 years. In 1994 he "wrestled" with God for some period of months and in September of that year totally surrendered his life to Jesus.

In 1996 he was so driven to study God's Word that he attended the Indianapolis campus of Trinity Evangelical Divinity School (Chicago) to earn a Certificate of Biblical Studies. His hunger for God's Word led him to lead and write all his own Bible studies for his small group. He has been a Bible study leader for the past 25 years.

After 25 years as an actuary, and 20 years as an entrepreneur, he began his third career as an author in 2020, when he published The OBSCURE Bible Study Series. The Jesus Follower Bible Study Series was completed in early 2025. He is a member of The Church at Station Hill in Spring Hill, TN, a regional campus of Brentwood Baptist (Brentwood TN).

"Get Wisdom Publishing is dedicated to being the trusted source of wisdom-driven books that inspire growth, guide decisions, and empower readers to live with purpose and fulfillment."

Contact Us

Website: www.getwisdompublishing.com

Email: info@getwisdompublishing.com

Facebook: Get Wisdom Publishing

Author's Page:
www.amazon.com/author/stephenhberkey

Amazon's Jesus Follower Bible Study Series page:
https://www.amazon.com/dp/B0DHP39P5J

*"Go beyond devotionals.
Experience biblical wisdom in action!"*

www.ingramcontent.com/pod-product-compliance
Lightning Source LLC
Chambersburg PA
CBHW060320050426
42449CB00011B/2566